CONVEYANCING

LAW & PRACTICE

TITLES IN THE SERIES

Business Law & Practice

Civil Litigation

Conveyancing Law & Practice

Criminal Litigation

Family Law & Practice

Intellectual Property with Competition Law & Practice

Introduction to the Legal Practice Course

Wills, Probate & Administration

CONVEYANCING
LAW & PRACTICE

Jennifer Mills, LLB, MA, Barrister
Principal Lecturer and Director of the Legal Practice Course
London Guildhall University

Judith Willis, BA, Solicitor
Senior Lecturer
London Guildhall University

London Guildhall-Cavendish
Legal Practice Course Companion Series

2ND EDITION

First published in Great Britain 1993 by Cavendish Publishing Limited, The Glass House, Wharton Street, London WC1X 9PX.

Telephone: 0171-278 8000 Facsimile: 0171-278 8080

British Library Cataloguing in Publication Data. A catalogue record for this book is available from the British Library.

ISBN 1-85941-004-9

Printed and bound in Great Britain

Contents

Table of cases

Table of statutes

Introduction

This companion has been written specifically for students studying on Legal Practice Courses and is intended as a companion to the workshops and exercises that you will undertake at your university or college. It does not include specimen documents or seek to work through imaginary transactions, as it is designed to complement the documentation and scenarios used within your own institution.

Our experience is that students find it difficult to handle both registered and unregistered and freehold and leasehold conveyancing simultaneously. Our aim is to ensure that you understand the basics before tackling more complex transactions.

Chapters 1–6 are of general application.

Chapters 7–13 then focus on the sale and purchase of a simple registered freehold title. Most residential conveyancing involves mortgages and co-ownership and these are therefore considered but less usual transactions are deferred until later.

Chapters 14–17 cover the sale and purchase of unregistered freeholds and in working through these chapters you will reinforce your understanding of basic freehold conveyancing.

Chapters 18–20 then introduce you to more complex transactions such as sales by personal representatives and through attorneys, sales of part and estate conveyancing.

At this stage you will be able to build on your knowledge of freehold conveyancing to tackle the additional issues involved in the granting and assigning of leases, which we cover in Chapters 21–25.

This approach, coupled with a direct straightforward style, will enable you to understand not only what has to be done at each stage of the transaction but also why it has to be done. It will enable you to see the conveyancing process not as a series of complex requirements but as a logical and coherent process.

Chapter 1

Introduction to conveyancing

What is conveyancing? 1.1

Conveyancing is real property law in action. It concerns the creation and transfer of estates and interests in land.

Note

It is important that you have a firm understanding of the principles of land law and the law of contract before tackling this subject.

Creation and transfer of estates 1.1.1

There are only two estates which can exist as legal estates:

- The *fee simple absolute in possession*; and
- The *term of years absolute*.

They tend to be referred to by the tenure on which they are held. The word 'legal' is not generally stated and 'title' is also frequently omitted. So the terms 'freehold' and 'leasehold' are widely used to mean respectively a legal fee simple estate held on freehold tenure and a legal term of years absolute held on leasehold tenure.

Creation of new estates 1.1.2

Freehold titles

It is *not* possible to create any new freehold titles except by subdividing an existing title. Where there is a sale of part of a title the buyer will be registered as the first proprietor of the title in that part and given a new title number.

The seller will remain as registered proprietor of the title in the retained land and will keep the old title number but the Property Register and filed plan will be amended to show that the area sold has been removed from that title.

Leasehold titles

A new leasehold title may be created out of a freehold title and a new sublease (underlease) out of a head lease. A sub-underlease may be created out of a sublease and theoretically the process can continue indefinitely with each sub-estate being for a shorter period than the estate out of which it is created.

The estate out of which a leasehold is created is called the reversionary estate, or superior title. When there is a sublease there will be both a freehold and a leasehold reversionary estate.

1.1.3 Transfer of existing estates

Existing freeholds, leases and subleases may be transferred as a result of:

- A contract of sale;
- A gift (which may be either a gift *inter vivos* or a gift taking effect on death);
- By operation of law, eg. on bankruptcy; or
- By court order.

Note

Most conveyancing transactions take place where there is a *sale* of land and this companion will be primarily concerned with sale and purchase transactions.

1.1.4 The sale and purchase of land

On a sale, the buyer will want to be satisfied that:

- The seller has the right to sell;
- They know about all third party interests in the land.

The seller's right to sell

The seller will have to prove title to the estate that is the subject of the sale.

If the title to the estate is *registered* this can easily be done by obtaining an official copy, known as an *office copy*, of the entries on the Land Register. This will show who is registered as proprietor of the title.

If the title is *unregistered* it will be more complex. The title will have to be traced back through the title deeds to a good *root of title* which is at least 15 years old (*see* Chapter 14).

Knowledge about all third party interests in the land

Some third party rights are removable and the buyer, having discovered their existence, will take the necessary steps to ensure that they take free from them. For example, the buyer will not want to take the land subject to existing mortgages or Matrimonial Homes Act (MHA) rights and will therefore ensure that the seller removes them before completion or at least gives the buyer the means of securing their removal post-completion.

Similarly, the buyer will not want to take the land subject to the rights of beneficiaries under a trust and will ensure that such rights are overreached by paying the purchase money to at least two trustees or to a trust corporation.

Other third party rights, such as easements, covenants and local land charges are not normally removable, nor can they be overreached. The buyer takes subject to them and will therefore want full details of them before entering into the contract.

Thus, conveyancing largely involves:

- Ensuring that the seller has *title*, ie. the right to sell; and
- Checking for *third party incumbrances* to ensure that they are appropriately dealt with so that the buyer either takes free from them or is fully aware of those that will continue to bind the land.

Creation of new third party interests 1.1.5

New third party rights are most commonly created when land is sold, eg. the buyer creates a new mortgage over the land or enters into new covenants and easements. It is possible, however, for new third party rights to be created at other times, eg. the owner of an unincumbered estate may mortgage it, or grant a neighbour a right of way over the land, or enter into covenants with a neighbour affecting the use of the land.

Transfer of existing third party interests 1.1.6

When an estate is transferred, the benefit and burden of third party interests (incumbrances) affecting the estate will generally also be transferred.

Benefit

Some third party rights are personal, eg. a spouse's MHA rights and a beneficiary's rights under a trust. The benefit of these does not pass to anyone else. Others are designed to benefit specific land, eg. easements and covenants, and the benefit of these will pass with the dominant land.

Burden

Third party rights that have been protected as minor interests by registration will generally bind a buyer. However, the rights of beneficiaries under a trust for sale or strict settlement will not bind the buyer even if protected by registration (ie. by restriction or caution) if the overreaching machinery is utilised. Others may be removable by the seller, eg. by repaying a mortgage loan, and so conveying the property unincumbered.

Third party rights in *registered land* which have *not* been registered will still bind the buyer if they qualify as *overriding interests*, eg. someone with the benefit of an estate contract who has failed to protect it as a minor interest by registering a notice or caution will, if in occupation at completion, gain alternative protection under s.70(1)(g), Land Registration Act (LRA) 1925.

If the title is *unregistered*, third party rights which are not registrable under the Land Charges Act (LCA) 1972 will be binding if they constitute legal interests or interests whose enforceability depends on the doctrine of notice, eg. pre-1926 restrictive covenants, and the buyer has notice of them. Rights which are capable or registration under the LCA but which have not been registered will not bind a purchaser of the legal estate even if the purchaser knows of them.

1.2 This companion

This companion deals only with residential (domestic) conveyancing. Commercial conveyancing is not included.

Figure 1.1 Main differences between registered and unregistered conveyancing

Registered	*Unregistered*
Checking that the seller has title to the property	
Inspect the Land Register to see who is registered as proprietor and what class of title they have.	Investigate title back through the deeds to a good root of title at least 15 years old.
Checking for third party incumbrances	
Inspect the Land Register to check for minor interests protected by entry on the Register.	Undertake a central land charges search to check for registered third party interests.
Check for overriding interests.	Check for other non-registrable interests which, if legal, will be binding and, if equitable, will be binding if the buyer has notice of them.
Search for local land charges.	Search for local land charges.
Registration of the transfer	
A disposition of a registered title must be registered otherwise the legal estate does not pass.	On completion legal title passes but if the transaction triggers compulsory registration, an application must be made to the Land Registry for first registration within two months of completion – otherwise legal title reverts to the seller: s.123, LRA 1925.

You will, however, be able to utilise the skills and knowledge gained in studying residential conveyancing in other contexts and you will acquire an understanding of the conveyancing process which will be transferrable to commercial conveyancing.

Stages in the conveyancing process 1.3

A sale and purchase of land falls into three phases:

- Up to exchange of contracts;
- Exchange to completion;
- Post-completion.

Up to exchange of contracts 1.3.1

This stage includes:

- Taking *instructions* to act for seller or buyer;
- Organising the *financial aspects* of the transaction;
- Drafting/approving the *contract of sale;*
- Checking that the seller has *title to the property*. In modern conveyancing this is usually done pre-exchange (*see* 1.4);
- Carrying out various *searches and enquiries* to enable the buyer to discover:
  - the physical state of the property;
  - third party rights affecting the land; and
  - other matters which may influence a buyer's decision whether or not to buy, eg. whether there are disputes with the neighbours or whether there are plans for new roads in the area;
- The *exchange of contracts*. Until this occurs either party may withdraw from the transaction without any liability to the other side. Once contracts have been exchanged, both sides are legally bound to complete, ie. to perform the contract – the buyer by paying the agreed price and the seller by transferring the agreed property.

Exchange to completion 1.3.2

This stage includes:

- Preparing the document necessary to *transfer the property*. This will be a Land Registry transfer (registered title), or deed of conveyance (unregistered title). (If the buyer is buying with the aid of a mortgage, the mortgage documentation will also have to be prepared.)
- Conducting certain *pre-completion searches* to check that there are no new third party rights/incumbrances;

- Ensuring that the *finance* is in place;
- *Completion* by payment of the price and the execution and handing over of the transfer/conveyance plus various other documents. (This is the performance of the contract, ie. the equivalent of the delivery of the goods under a sale of goods contract.)

1.3.3 Post-completion

To validate the transaction and ensure that the buyer gets legal title to the estate purchased, you must take the following steps:

- *Stamp* the transfer/conveyance;
- *Registration* – either registration of the dealing if the title was already registered or first registration if it was previously an unregistered title.

1.3.4 Stages in a freehold conveyancing transaction

Seller	*Buyer*
Take instructions.	Take instructions.
Investigate title and prepare draft contract.	Organise survey and finance, and await draft contract.
	Make local and special searches.
If Protocol is followed, supply buyer with fixtures, fittings and contents form and property information form.	Check what is supplied and make any further enquiries as necessary.
Deduce title.	Investigate title.
Negotiation of changes to the draft contract.	
Receipt of approved draft.	Approve draft contract.
Exchange of contracts	
Deduce title if not done pre-exchange.	Investigate title.
Approve purchase deed.	Prepare purchase deed.
Preparation for completion.	Preparation for completion.
Completion	
Post-completion matters.	Post-completion matters.

1.4 The National Conveyancing Protocol

There are certain aspects of the traditional conveyancing process which may give rise to delay or difficulty. The National Conveyancing Protocol was introduced by the Law Society in the hope of speeding up the pre-exchange stage and reducing the possibility of problems arising after contracts have been exchanged which might delay completion or even entitle the buyer to withdraw from the contract.

The protocol is known as the TransAction scheme. This is its marketing name and the TransAction logo appears on the documentation used when following the Protocol. When first introduced in 1990 the Protocol sought to place on the seller the responsibility for providing the buyer with the results of the local search. This was not generally acceptable to sellers and this and the fact that local authorities have reduced the time taken to provide the results of local searches, have resulted in the 3rd (1994) edition of the Protocol abandoning this step. The Protocol is therefore now achieving wider acceptance.

The Protocol is a form of best practice and the Council of the Law Society recommends its use in all domestic conveyancing transactions.

Note

Every solicitor is required to notify the solicitor acting for the other party whether or not the Protocol will be used and also of any subsequent decision to depart from it.

Main differences: traditional conveyancing and the Protocol 1.4.1

Pre-contract enquiries

Traditionally, it is for the buyer to initiate certain pre-contract enquiries of the seller. Some buyers' solicitors like to make pages and pages of enquiries regardless of whether they are relevant to the particular property. These are very time consuming to answer and may delay the exchange of contracts.

Under the Protocol, the seller assembles a 'property package', which includes a property information form, giving replies to the standard questions which buyers always ask. Buyers' solicitors are then encouraged only to make additional enquiries which are necessary to clarify points that have arisen out of the documents which the seller has provided or which are relevant to the particular property eg. because of its type or location.

As well as the property information form, the package contains a 'fixtures, fittings and contents' form clarifying which items are included in and which excluded from the sale.

If the package can be made available to the buyer with the draft contract or soon after, the pre-contract stage should be simplified.

Deducing title

Traditionally, title is not deduced by the seller until *after* the exchange of contracts. If it then transpires that the seller's title is defective and that the seller cannot transfer what they contracted to sell, the buyer will be entitled to withdraw from the contract. This will be very inconvenient, especially if the parties are in the middle of a chain transaction.

Where the title is *registered*, the process of deducing title is simple, ie. by providing copies of the entries on the Register. Hence, even before the introduction of the Protocol it was common practice for registered titles to be deduced pre-exchange. However, with *unregistered* titles the traditional process is sometimes still followed.

Under the Protocol, title is always *deduced by the seller* and *investigated by the buyer* before contracts are exchanged.

Terminology

The Protocol sought to make the conveyancing process more user-friendly by adopting the terms 'seller' and 'buyer' in place of the traditional 'vendor' and 'purchaser'. This change in terminology is also found in the Standard Conditions of Sale (*see* Chapter 8) which were introduced at the same time as the Protocol but which can be, and are, used even when the Protocol is not being followed.

Note, however, that the terms 'buyer' and 'purchaser' are not synonymous. Many statutory provisions protect a 'purchaser' and s.205, Law of Property Act (LPA) 1925 defines a purchaser to include a lessee, mortgagee or other person who for valuable consideration acquires an interest in the property. When dealing with such statutory provisions the term 'purchaser' must therefore still be used and it cannot be replaced with 'buyer'.

Self-assessment questions

1 What is the significance of the exchange of contracts?

2 What are the two main legal issues which the buyer's solicitor is employed to investigate?

3 What is the National Conveyancing Protocol?

4 What are the two main differences between a transaction following the traditional pattern and one where the Protocol is adopted?

Chapter 2

The Land Register

The form of the Land Register 2.1

There is no central land register but a number of district land registries, where titles to land served by each district registry are registered.

More than one title can be registered in a piece of land; where the land is subject to a lease the freehold title, the leasehold title and any sub-leasehold title will all be separately registered. Each title will have a separate title number and separate register.

The Register is divided into three parts:

- The Property Register;
- The Proprietorship Register;
- The Charges Register.

The Property Register 2.1.1

This gives a brief description of the property and refers to the Land Registry plan, called the *filed plan*, which exists for each registered title. It states whether the title is freehold or leasehold.

If *leasehold*, it will give brief particulars of the lease, the length of the term and the rent, but not its full terms. If the superior title is registered, it will give its title number.

> *Note*
>
> The lease itself remains an essential title document in any dealing with the leasehold title.

If the property enjoys the benefit of rights of way over neighbouring land, these are sometimes expressly stated in this part of the Register but, even if they are not mentioned, the proprietor will still be entitled to all appurtenant rights.

The Proprietorship Register 2.1.2

This states the class of title. This may be:

- Absolute;
- Possessory;
- Qualified; or
- Good leasehold.

The Register gives the names and addresses of the registered proprietors. Up to four persons can be registered as proprietors and up to three addresses may be given for each.

Note

It is important that proprietors keep the Land Registry informed of any change of address as, should the Land Registry need to communicate with the registered proprietors, it will do so at the addresses listed.

It is in this part of the Register that inhibitions, restrictions and cautions appear. These are all devices for protecting minor interests.

Sometimes the Land Registry notes other matters here, eg. where a proprietor has given an indemnity in respect of pre-existing covenants it may be noted here to remind the proprietor, when they come to sell, to take an indemnity from their transferee.

2.1.3 The Charges Register

This part of the Register records registered charges, ie. legal mortgages, and notices protecting minor interests.

2.1.4 The filed plan

After the Charges Register there is a copy of the filed plan. This is based on the Ordnance Survey map for the area and marks in red the property in question.

2.2 Protection of minor interests

All minor interests need to be protected by entry on the Register. There are four different devices for doing so:

- Inhibitions;
- Restrictions;
- Cautions;
- Notices.

2.2.1 Inhibitions

An inhibition is entered in the Proprietorship Register by the court or by the Chief Land Registrar.

The principal type is a *bankruptcy inhibition*. This is entered where a bankruptcy order has been made against a registered proprietor. It prevents the proprietor dealing with the title.

Note

A bankruptcy inhibition is usually preceded by a creditor's notice which is entered when a bankruptcy petition has been lodged against a registered proprietor.

Most *notices* appear in the Charges Register but a creditor's notice is an exception and appears in the Proprietorship Register.

Restrictions 2.2.2

Restrictions are entered in the *Proprietorship Register* at the request of the proprietor.

Where the proprietor is a corporation a restriction may indicate the particular officers of the corporation who are authorised to act on its behalf.

Where the registered proprietor is a *tenant for life* under a settlement, a restriction will indicate this and give the names of the trustees of the settlement to whom any purchase money will have to be paid.

Where there is more than one registered proprietor they will hold on *trust for sale*. A restriction in the following terms is sometimes entered:

> No disposition by one proprietor of the land (being the survivor of joint proprietors and not being a trust corporation) under which capital money arises is to be registered except under an order of the Registrar or of the court.

This restriction will be entered where the proprietors are holding as beneficial tenants in common. It will ensure that a purchaser does not deal with the sole survivor alone but insists on the appointment of second trustee so as to overreach the deceased's beneficial interest.

This restriction will *not* appear where the proprietors are holding as beneficial joint tenants because the right of survivorship will then apply to both the legal and equitable titles and the sole surviving trustee will therefore be entitled to deal with the property alone.

Where the proprietors hold as *beneficial joint tenants* and, in consequence, no restriction is entered, it is essential that if they subsequently sever the beneficial tenancy application be made to the Registry for the entry of the restriction. Severance can be effected unilaterally by one tenant simply serving notice of severance on the other(s). If the restriction is not entered, then any purchaser is entitled to assume that they have continued as beneficial joint tenants and that the survivor can deal with the property alone.

Note

Where there is no co-ownership restriction a purchaser must still be alert to the possibility of someone else, who is not a registered proprietor, having a beneficial interest. If they were to be in occupation at completion their beneficial interest would constitute an overriding interest under s.70(1)(g) LRA 1925 and therefore the purchaser would have to ensure that the purchase money was paid to at least two trustees.

2.2.3 Cautions

A caution against dealing can be entered in the *Proprietorship Register* by a third party to protect their interest.

Note

The main device for protecting third party interests is the notice.

In contrast to registering a *notice*, registering a caution does not require production of the land certificate. Thus, the cooperation of the registered proprietor is unnecessary. A caution is therefore fundamentally a hostile entry.

A caution simply indicates the name of the cautioner and the date it is lodged. This contrasts with a notice which indicates the type of interest it is intended to protect.

The cautioner has the right to be notified by the Land Registry of any application made to register a dealing with the property or to make any entry on the Register. The cautioner can then appear before the Registrar to assert their interest and, if it is established, the application for registration will be made subject to the cautioner's right.

A caution can be 'warned off' at any time. This means that the registered proprietor requires the Land Registry to give the cautioner 14 days within which to substantiate their right. If the cautioner fails to do so the caution will be removed.

The 'warning-off' mechanism prevents the title being clogged by unsubstantiated third party entries. The existence of a caution against the title will impede any dealing with the title as prospective purchasers will not be prepared to proceed until they have details of and are satisfied as to the right protected by the caution. Usually they will require its removal before they will proceed.

Note

An improperly lodged caution will entitle the registered proprietor to claim compensation for any resulting loss.

2.2.4 Notices

Notices are entered in the *Charges Register* to protect minor interests such as leases, restrictive covenants, estate contracts, rights under the Matrimonial Homes Act 1983, equitable mortgages and equitable easements.

To enter a notice the land certificate held by the registered proprietor must generally be produced. The most important exception is a notice of a spouse's right of occupation under the MHA. As production of the land certificate is not required, this type of notice can be entered as a hostile entry.

A creditor's notice and a notice of a lease at a rent without a fine, ie. without a premium, can also be entered without production of the land certificate.

Note

If a registered charge exists, the Land Registry will already hold the land certificate. The charge certificate held by the chargee will only have to be produced to register a notice if the notice adversely affects the chargee's title.

Where a notice protects a right of which there are lengthy details, these are usually set out in a separate schedule to the Charges Register. This commonly arises where there are restrictive covenants. Thus, following the Charges Register, there may be a schedule of several pages setting out details of the covenants.

Land and charge certificates 2.3

When the title is registered, the proprietor is issued with a land certificate which contains a copy of the entries on the Register. This has to be produced to the Land Registry to register any disposition of the property and for the entry of restrictions and most notices – but not for the entry of a caution or inhibition. The land certificate may therefore not show the up to date state of the Register. It can be sent to the registry at any time for updating and the date on which the certificate was last compared with the Register is stamped inside the front cover of the certificate.

When you need to know the current state of the title you should not rely on the entries in the land certificate as they may be out of date. You should obtain from the Land Registry an official copy of the current entries on the Register. These are known as *office copies*.

If there is a registered charge, ie. a legal charge in existence, the land certificate is kept by the Land Registry and only returned to the registered proprietor when all registered charges have been discharged. The chargee is issued with a charge certificate in its place. This is very similar to a land certificate in that it contains a copy of the entries on the Register as at the date of issue of the certificate but it also contains the original mortgage deed. If a second mortgage is created that too will be registered in the Charges Register and the chargee issued with a certificate of second charge which includes a copy of the entries on the Register and the original second mortgage deed.

2.4 Inspecting the Register

Since 3 December 1990 the Land Register has been open to the public and anyone can obtain details of any title by applying for a set of office copies.

If you do not know the title number of the land in which you are interested, you can first apply for a search in the public index map. This will tell you whether or not a title in a particular piece of land is already registered and, if it is, the title number. You can then apply for a set of office copies of the title.

On a sale of a registered title, it is usual for the seller to send the buyer a set of up to date office copies with the draft contract. If, at a later date, you want to check whether there have been any new entries made on the Register, it is not necessary to obtain a fresh set of office copies. You simply apply for an official search of the Register, asking whether there have been new entries since the date of issue of the office copies.

If office copies or official search certificates are inaccurate, eg. if they fail to reveal something that was actually on the Register, then the purchaser will still be bound by the entry but will be entitled to seek compensation from the Land Registry: s.83, LRA 1925.

2.5 Registration of title

The present system of registration of title has existed since 1925 and has gradually been extended throughout the country by declaring areas to be compulsory registration areas. Compulsory registration of title was finally extended to the whole of England and Wales on 1 December 1990.

However, even where registration has been in force for many years, there are still some unregistered titles, as registration is only compulsory when certain events take place which require an application for first registration of title.

2.5.1 Compulsory registration

Following completion of any of the transactions listed below, the freehold title in (a) and the leasehold title in (b) and (c) must be registered within *two* months: s.123, Land Registration Act 1925.

(a) A conveyance on sale of the freehold;

(b) The grant of a lease for more than 21 years out of an unregistered freehold title;

(c) The assignment on sale of an unregistered lease with more than 21 years still to run at the date of the assignment.

Note

In situations (b) and (c) it is only the lease which is being granted or assigned which has to be registered. The superior reversionary title may remain unregistered until it is itself dealt with in circumstances rendering registration compulsory.

Registration is also compulsory where a lease for more than 21 years is granted out of a registered freehold title. This constitutes a disposition of an existing registered title and such a lease is consequently called a dispositionary lease. The two-month time limit for registration under s.123 does not apply in this case but the lessee only acquires legal title when the title is registered; not on the granting of the lease.

Completing the Register 2.5.2

Voluntary registration can be applied for at any time.

The more recently the area became an area of compulsory registration the higher will be the proportion of remaining unregistered titles. In rural areas there is still a high but, with compulsory registration, progressively diminishing percentage of unregistered titles.

At the end of 1992 there were nearly 14 million registered titles, approximately two-thirds of the estimated number of separate titles in England and Wales. The Land Registry is considering strategies for speeding up the process of registration of the remaining unregistered titles and completing the Register. The amendment of s.123 to provide new 'trigger mechanisms' for compulsory registration is the most likely method.

Registration may become compulsory whenever there is a change of ownership even if it does not occur 'on sale'. If there is a sale of part of an unregistered title, only the part sold has to be registered at present and the part retained can remain unregistered. This might change. Ways of encouraging public bodies, whose land rarely change hands, to register title voluntarily are also under consideration. However, for some years to come, conveyancers will have to deal with unregistered titles from time to time and those who can do so with confidence will be in demand.

Self-assessment questions

1. What is the difference between the Property Register, the Proprietorship Register and the Charges Register?
2. What are minor interests and will they bind a buyer?
3. What is the difference between a land certificate and a charge certificate?
4. Registration of title is now compulsory throughout England and Wales; so why do unregistered titles still exist?

Chapter 3

Taking instructions

Obtaining instructions and information 3.1

If a seller or buyer wishes you to act on a sale or purchase, you will have to take instructions from the client. Often you will be acting for a person who is both selling and buying and will therefore need to take instructions on *both* transactions.

The solicitor as agent 3.1.1

A solicitor acts as *agent* for the client and must therefore act within the authority (mandate) given by the client (the principal). You must never accept instructions to do anything which is illegal or which would constitute a breach of the rules of professional practice for example, the:

- Solicitors' Practice Rules;
- Solicitors' Accounts Rules;
- Solicitors' Publicity Code.

Note

These matters are considered in detail in Chapter 5 and in the Law Society's *Guide to the Professional Conduct of Solicitors*. They *must* be followed at all stages of the conveyancing transaction.

There are certain things that the solicitor will have *implied authority* to do unless otherwise instructed, eg. to effect an exchange of contracts by any usual method.

Be thorough 3.1.2

You must obtain clear and precise instructions as to what your client wishes and authorises you to do and all the information you will need to carry through those instructions. You must keep your client informed as to the progress you are making throughout the transaction.

Matters may arise on which you will need to obtain further instructions but, if you obtain full instructions and information at the outset, this should reduce the need to keep having to refer back to your client.

Giving explanation and advice 3.2

When taking instructions you will be asked to explain the transaction, or specific aspects of it, to your client and to give advice; in particular:

- *General explanation* of the sale/purchase process – what you will be doing for your client, what they will need to do themselves, the various stages in the transaction, especially the significance of exchange of contracts and of completion;
- How *long* it is likely to take;
- The *costs* of the transaction;
- The *financing* of the purchase – this may include general financial services advice and advice on types of mortgage and on mortgage interest relief;
- Explanation of the differences between *joint tenancy* and *tenancy in common* and which is appropriate to the clients' circumstances;
- On a sale, advice on possible *capital gains tax* liability.

3.3 Taking instructions from a seller

3.3.1 Checklist

(a) Names, addresses, telephone numbers (home and work) of seller(s).

Capacity in which they are selling, ie. is it their own property or are they selling, for example, as a personal representative or agent.

(b) Details of buyer(s) and their solicitor if known.

(c) Was the sale arranged through an estate agent? If so, obtain the estate agent's name, address and telephone number and a copy of their particulars.

Is there a particular person with whom the seller has been dealing?

Ascertain what arrangements the client has made with the agent regarding commission and whether, if the sale goes through, the client will wish you to settle the agent's bill directly out of the proceeds of sale.

(d) Details of the property:

- Address
- Freehold/leasehold
- Registered/unregistered – the whereabouts of the title deeds, or the land or charge certificate.

Get the client to complete the property information form.

(e) Does the seller have a mortgage on the property? If so, obtain details of the mortgagee and the account number and an estimate from the client of the amount outstanding on the mortgage. Check whether there are subsequent mortgages on the property and, if so, obtain similar details of them.

(f) The price – what does it include?

- Are any fixtures to be removed?
- Are any chattels being sold? If so, are they included in the price or to be purchased for a separate consideration?
- Get the client to complete the fixtures, fittings and contents form.
- Has any preliminary deposit been paid by the buyer? If so, to whom?

(g) Obtain instructions regarding the proceeds of sale.

(h) Is there a related purchase? If so, you will need to synchronise the exchange of contracts and generally have the same completion date on both contracts so that your client can move straight from one property to the other.

If the purchase is dependant on the sale proceeds, then you must ensure that completion of the sale takes place earlier in the day so that the proceeds are available for the purchase.

(i) Does the client have any objection to your letting the other side know that there is a related transaction and the progress on it?

(j) Completion date – what target date would the client like you to work towards?

(k) Ask for any correspondence that exists between the client and the prospective buyer and with any other party involved.

(l) Are there any other special instructions that you require, given the circumstances of the case, or other issues that the client wishes to raise?

Action following instructions 3.3.2

(a) Confirm instructions in writing to the client and to the other side. Advise the other side whether or not you intend to follow the Protocol.

(b) Obtain the charge certificate(s) from the mortgagee(s) by giving an undertaking (*see* Chapter 5, para. 5.8.1).

(c) Obtain a set of office copy entries from the district land registry (*see* Chapter 8, para. 8.3.2).

(d) Examine the seller's title and then draft the contract.

(e) Send the buyer:

- Two copies of the draft contract;
- Office copy entries;

and if the Protocol is being followed:

- The property information form;
- The fixtures, fittings and contents form.

3.4 Taking instructions from a buyer

3.4.1 Checklist

(a) Names, addresses, phone numbers (home and work) of buyer(s).

Capacity in which they are buying, eg. on their own or with others.

(b) Details of seller(s) and their solicitor, if known.

(c) Was purchase arranged through an estate agent? If so, obtain the estate agent's name, address and telephone number, a copy of their particulars and the name of any person with whom the client has been dealing.

(d) Details of the property:

- Address
- Freehold/leasehold
- Type and age
- Location.

You need to be able to visualise the sort of property your client is buying.

(e) The price – what does it include? Has any preliminary deposit been paid by the buyer? If so, to whom?

(f) How is the purchase to be financed? It may be necessary to give the client advice on sources and types of mortgage finance (*see* Chapter 4, para. 4.3).

(g) If there are more than two purchasers, how are they going to hold the beneficial title? Advice will need to be given on the two forms of co-ownership and the advantages and disadvantages of each and which is more appropriate to the clients' circumstances, but the first interview is probably not the best time to discuss this in detail.

Note

If a conflict of interest arises between the purchasers then they must seek separate advice on this point (*see* Chapter 5, para. 5.4.4).

(h) Is there a related sale? If so, it will be essential to synchronise the exchange of contracts on the two transactions and the completion dates will normally need to coincide?

(i) Does the client have any objection to your letting the other side know that there is a related transaction and the progress on it?

(j) Completion date – what target date would the client like you to work towards?

(k) Ask for any correspondence that exists between the client and the prospective seller and with any other party involved.

(l) Are there any other special instructions that you require, given the circumstances of the case, or other issues that the client wishes to raise?

Action following instructions 3.4.2

(a) Confirm instructions in writing to the client and to the other side. Confirm adoption of Protocol if appropriate.

(b) Ensure that the client progresses the mortgage application and any separate survey that the client has decided is to be done.

(c) Institute a local land charges search and enquiries of the local authority, plus any other appropriate searches (*see* Chapter 9).

(d) Await receipt from the seller of the draft contract and, if the Protocol is being followed, the property package. If the Protocol is not being followed, make preliminary enquiries of the seller.

Self-assessment questions

1 What is the legal relationship between a solicitor and client, and what governs the terms of that relationship?

2 On what particular issue will you need to advise co-purchasers?

3 When acting for a client who is both selling and buying, what particular problem will you face?

4 Clients frequently ask how long the transaction will take. How will you reply?

Chapter 4

Financial aspects

Costs of the transaction 4.1

Quoting on costs 4.1.1

This may form part of the initial interview with the client when you take instructions but may well arise at an earlier stage when a potential client asks for a quote before deciding whether or not to instruct you. Do not be so anxious to get the instruction that you quote an uneconomic rate.

Solicitors' fees 4.1.2

There are no fixed (scale) fees for solicitors' conveyancing charges. Solicitors are free to charge what they think the market will bear.

Over the past decade conveyancing fees have not increased, so in real terms they have fallen considerably. Indeed in many cases they have actually fallen and solicitors today are charging less than they were 10 years ago. Cut-price conveyancing is widely available and is causing considerable concern. It is feared that when charging very low fees conveyancers may have to cut corners and that negligence may result. Another problem is that conveyancing, which traditionally subsidised certain other areas of practice, eg. legal aid work, no longer provides a reasonable fee income. The recent long recession in the property market has greatly exacerbated such problems.

It is important to distinguish between a fixed quote, which cannot be increased if the job turns out to be more complex than anticipated, and an estimate which, subject to certain procedures, can be revised.

Solicitors' fees attract VAT at 17½%. When quoting on costs you must always make it absolutely clear that VAT will be added to your fees.

Items such as telephone calls and photocopying are not generally charged for separately but are included in the overall fee. However, if they are charged for separately they will also be subject to VAT as they constitute the provision of services by you.

Note

Telegraphic Transfer (TT) charges for transmitting funds on completion from the buyer's solicitor's client account to the seller's solicitor's client account are often charged for separately and VAT will be payable on them.

4.1.3 Disbursements

During the transaction you will pay out various items of expenditure on your client's behalf such as stamp duty, Land Registry fees, and search fees. These items will feature on your bill as disbursements and will not attract VAT.

4.1.4 Other items of expenditure

There will be a number of other expenses which a client will need to take into account, eg. estate agent's fees and removal costs. These will often be payable by the client directly to the payee, eg. a survey fee payable to the mortgagee.

Note

See Chapter 5, para. 5.3 for the professional conduct issues regarding costs.

4.1.5 Typical costs

The following table of costs is for *illustration only*. There is considerable variation in solicitors', mortgagees', surveyors' and estate agents' fees, and Land Registry registration fees and search fees are subject to frequent change.

Assume that your client is selling a property for £80,000 and buying another for £120,000. There is a £30,000 mortgage outstanding on the property being sold and a mortgage of £70,000 will be taken out on the new house.

Sales costs

1	Estate agent's fees, say 2% (could be more)	1,600.00
	+ VAT	280.00
2	Solicitor's fees	250.00
	+ VAT	43.75
3	Office copy entries including filed plan	10.00
4	Possibly a mortgagee's administrative charge, say	50.00
		2,233.75

Purchase costs

1	Solicitor's fees	300.00
	+ VAT	52.50
2	Stamp Duty at 1%	1,200.00
3	Land Registry registration fee (This is on a scale depending on the amount of the consideration.)	230.00

4	Search fees	
	Local search (variable)	80.00
	Land Registry search	5.00
	Bankruptcy search (if two buyers)	2.00
5	Telegraphic transfer	25.00
	+VAT	4.38
6	Possibly a mortgagee's administrative charge, say	100.00
7	Survey costs (variable and depends on type of survey, eg. basic valuation survey £60–70, home buyer's survey £200, full structural survey 1% of the value of the property).	200.00
	+ VAT	35.00
		2,233.88

Overall budget

Sale price	80,000.00
Less outstanding mortgage	30,000.00
	50,000.00
Less costs of sale	2,233.75
Balance of sale proceeds	47,766.25
Purchase price	120,000.00
Plus costs	2,233.88
	122,233.88
Less mortgage advance	70,000.00
	52,233.88
Less sale proceeds	47,766.25
Balance required from client	4,467.63

Note

Possible retentions from the mortgage advance, the possible costs of reconnecting services, eg. the telephone line to the property, and removal costs have been ignored.

Mortgagee's administrative charges

These are a very variable but increasingly common item. On a sale there may be an administrative charge levied in connection with the redemption of the mortgage. This should not be confused with a penalty interest payment which the seller/mortgagor may have to pay where they redeem a fixed term mortgage early. Mortgagees sometimes have a discretion to waive charges where the mortgagor is taking out a mortgage on the new property with the same mortgagee.

On a purchase the new mortgagee may charge an 'arrangement fee' for setting up the mortgage. Building society charges are generally moderate but banks frequently charge at least 1% of the amount of the loan. If the mortgagee is separately represented, their solicitor's fees plus VAT will also have to be met by the buyer. These may be considerable.

4.2 Stamp duty

The levying of stamp duty on certain documents is a means by which the government raises revenue. At one time there were many conveyancing and non-conveyancing documents that attracted stamp duty but over the years it became increasingly not cost-effective to collect small amounts of duty, eg. at one time all receipts had to have a 2d (ie. two *old* pence) duty, and many stamp duties have been abolished.

In conveyancing large sums of money are involved and there is consequently scope for the government to raise substantial amounts by way of stamp duty. All transfers on sale of either freeholds or leaseholds are subject to stamp duty at 1% of the consideration but if the consideration does not exceed £60,000 and the transfer contains a certificate of value to that effect then a nil duty will be charged.

The certificate of value will say:

> It is hereby certified that the transaction hereby effected does not form part of a larger transaction or of a series of transactions in respect of which the amount or value or the aggregate amount or value of the consideration exceeds £60,000.

Note the reference here to *series* of transactions. It is *not* possible to sell a property worth £100,000 by transferring it in two halves for £50,000 each and by inserting a certificate of value in each transfer pay nil duty.

If the transfer does not contain a certificate of value, duty at 1% will be payable even though the consideration does not in fact exceed £60,000.

Note

Where duty is payable it is payable on the full amount of the consideration and not just on the amount over £60,000, eg. if the price is £70,000 then the stamp duty will be £700. If the price is £60,001 the duty will be £601.

Where chattels are being sold it may be preferable to buy them for a separate consideration rather than including them in the price of the land. This may save stamp duty as duty is only payable on the consideration paid for the land. Any figure put on the chattels must be reasonable. Overvaluing the chattels would constitute a fraud on the Inland Revenue.

The principal Act governing the payment of stamp duty is the Stamp Act 1891 but the rate of stamp duty and the point at which the nil band operates is varied from time to time by annual Finance Acts. At one time the basic rate of stamp duty was 2% but then there were lower bands of 1½%, 1% and ½% as well as a nil band. You will therefore find when looking back at old conveyances that the amount of duty that has been paid is not necessarily 1% of the consideration. You will also find certificates of value referring not to £60,000 but to a variety of other figures that were of significance at the time in order to determine the rate of duty that was then payable.

A document which attracts stamp duty should be stamped within 30 days of its execution. Late stamping is possible but a penalty may be payable.

A document that requires stamping is inadmissible in evidence if unstamped. It will not be a good root or link in a chain of title to unregistered land and, most importantly, it will not be accepted for registration by the Land Registry.

Stamping of leases 4.2.1

On the sale of an existing lease the stamp duty position is exactly the same as on the sale of a freehold. However, when a lease is first granted the stamping position is different because duty is assessed not only on the premium, ie. the lump sum that the lessee initially pays to acquire the lease, but also on the annual rent.

The premium will attract duty at 1% but if it does not exceed £60,000 a certificate of value to claim the benefit of the nil band can be inserted but only if the amount of the rent does not exceed £600 *per annum*.

On the rent the amount of duty will depend not only on the amount of the rent but also on the length of the lease. The longer the lease the higher the rate of duty will be. Bear in mind, however, that long leases are generally granted for a substantial premium and a comparatively small annual ground rent.

When a lease is granted there will be two identical documents – the lease and the counterpart lease. The *lease* is executed by the lessor and handed to the lessee and it is the lessee's responsibility to stamp it in accordance with the above rules. The *counterpart lease* is executed by the lessee and handed to the lessor. The counterpart attracts a fixed rate stamp duty of 50p and it is the lessor's responsibility to stamp it.

4.2.2 Voluntary conveyances

A conveyance by way of gift at one time attracted stamp duty on the market value of the property. Such conveyances had to be sent to the Inland Revenue for adjudication, ie. for the Inland Revenue to determine the value of the property and therefore the amount of duty payable. Since 1 May 1987 such transfers are exempt from duty provided they contain the following certificate:

It is certified that the transaction hereby effected falls within Category L in the Schedule to the Stamp Duty (Exempt Instruments) Regulations 1987.

4.3 Mortgage finance

The two main sources of mortgage finance are banks and building societies. As institutional lenders their mortgage requirements and documentation will be well worked out and a solicitor acting for them will receive precise instructions on their requirements.

There are two principal types of mortgage:

- An ordinary repayment mortgage;
- A mortgage coupled with an endowment policy.

4.3.1 Repayment mortgage

In the ordinary repayment mortgage the mortgagor not only pays the mortgagee interest on the loan but also makes repayments of capital, so that throughout the life of the mortgage the capital outstanding will gradually be reduced. At the end of the term, eg. at the end of 25 years, the mortgage debt will be paid off.

In the early years of the mortgage the monthly payments that the mortgagor makes will primarily be interest payments and the capital element being repaid will be small, but as the years pass the proportion of capital to interest being paid each month will increase.

Mortgage protection insurance

In the case of a *repayment mortgage*, on the death of the mortgagor the remaining capital sum will still be outstanding and the mortgagor's estate will remain liable for the debt. It will probably be necessary to sell the mortgaged property in order for the estate to discharge this debt. If the mortgagor has no dependants who will be prejudiced by this it may not be a matter of concern but generally it is advisable in the case of a repayment mortgage for the mortgagor to take out a life insurance policy.

This will not be an endowment insurance which will, should the mortgagor survive for a fixed period of years, mature and provide a capital sum, but a life policy which is only payable in the event of the mortgagor's death. It may be taken out for the life assured's life (a whole life policy) or just for the duration of the mortgage term (term insurance). Both are relatively cheap forms of life insurance. With term insurance, if the mortgagor survives for the full term of the mortgage, the policy produces nothing. In order to keep premiums low, such policies frequently secure only the declining balance of the mortgage debt.

Note

A life insurance policy which covers the mortgagor if the mortgagor dies is known as a mortgage protection policy. These can also be taken out to provide cover where the mortgagor at some future time is unable, through redundancy or ill health, to keep up the mortgage payments. Insurance against these risks is advisable for both repayment and endowment mortgages.

Endowment mortgage 4.3.2

In an endowment mortgage the mortgagor makes payments to the mortgagee of interest only. At the end of the mortgage term of the full capital sum is still owing. This, however, is repaid out of the proceeds of a life insurance policy that the mortgagor will have taken out at the time of the granting of the mortgage.

This obviously means that throughout the mortgage term the mortgagor will not only be paying interest on the mortgage debt but will also be paying life insurance premiums. At one time these too were eligible for tax relief.

Note

As a result of the abolition of tax relief on premiums, endowment mortgages are less common than they were, particularly for older purchasers when premiums will be higher and alternative investments may be more attractive.

Payment of the policy monies

Under endowment insurance the policy monies become payable:

- When the policy matures after the specified number of years for which it is taken out; or
- On the death of the life assured should that happen earlier.

If, therefore, the mortgagor dies during the mortgage term their family will not be left with the outstanding mortgage debt to repay as it will be paid off from the proceeds of the endowment policy.

The capital sum

There are many different forms of life insurance policy on the market and a borrower needs to ensure that the policy taken out will provide a guaranteed capital sum at the end of the mortgage term.

In recent years many people have taken out so-called *low-cost endowment mortgages* that are based on an anticipated capital value at the end of the term. Where the insurance company's investments have not performed as well as anticipated this has resulted in these policies not producing at maturity the anticipated capital sum. Borrowers in such circumstances find themselves left with a shortfall where the amount of the insurance policy does not pay off the amount of the mortgage debt.

Charging the policy

In the case of an endowment linked mortgage, the mortgagee may take a charge over the life insurance policy, in which case there will be two charges involved in the mortgage transaction:

- A charge over the land; and
- A charge over the life policy.

A charge over the life policy is created by *assigning the benefit* of the policy to the mortgagee in accordance with the Policies of Assurance Act 1867, which requires notice in writing of the assignment to be given to the insurance company. The company will then record that the mortgagee has rights in the policy and in the event of the policy monies becoming payable will make payment to the mortgagee.

If ever the mortgage is redeemed then, of course, the rights under the life policy need to be assigned back to the borrower. There will need to be a reassignment of the policy and a further notification to the life insurance company to let them know that the mortgagee no longer has any interest in the policy. The assignment of the policy and the reassignment both form part of the chain of title to the policy and *must* be retained with the policy.

Note

It is increasingly common for mortgagees not to bother to take an assignment of the life policy.

4.3.3 Selling mortgaged property

The mortgage when taken out will be planned to run for a

fixed period, eg. 25 years. However, most people do not stay in the same house for that length of time. The seller redeems the mortgage on the property they are selling out of the proceeds of the sale and takes a new mortgage on the property they are buying. The new mortgage may or may not be with the same bank or building society.

If they have an endowment mortgage on the old property then the same life insurance policy can be used as the basis for an endowment mortgage on the new property, although if the amount being raised by way of mortgage on the new property is greater than on the old property the amount of life insurance cover will need to be increased.

If the seller is not taking out a new mortgage, or if they wish to change to a repayment mortgage, they can if they wish surrender the endowment policy to the insurance company or sell it. People buy other people's endowment policies as an investment and this may produce a better price for the seller than cashing in the policy for its surrender value, especially if the policy has not been in force for very long and therefore has a low surrender value.

Mortgage interest relief 4.4

Tax relief is obtainable on certain mortgage interest payments in order to encourage home ownership. Interest on a loan for the purchase of land is eligible for relief if the property is the *only* or *main residence* of the borrower. The relief is granted on the interest payable on a loan of up to £30,000.

Note

The relief is not £30,000 per annum; it is a relief on the interest payable on £30,000.

In the case of institutional lenders, the relief is granted under the MIRAS (Mortgage Interest Relief At Source) Scheme. This means that the borrower does not pay the full rate of interest on the first £30,000 of their borrowing but pays the mortgagee the *net* interest, ie. the gross interest less the tax relief, and the mortgagee reclaims the tax from the Revenue.

The rate at which the relief is granted has been progressively reduced and as from April 1995 the rate is £15%.

Note

Before 1 August 1988 when two or more people purchased a property jointly they could each claim the benefit of the full mortgage interest relief but on loans taken out since then the relief is only £30,000 *per property*.

If a buyer is not already utilising their full mortgage interest relief on an existing property and they borrow in order to pay the deposit on a new property then the interest on that borrowing for the deposit will be eligible for relief provided the money is borrowed on a loan account rather than simply as an overdraft facility.

4.5 Financial services

Any person carrying on investment business must be authorised under the Financial Services Act 1986.

Investment business does *not* include generic advice on whether a repayment or an endowment mortgage is the more suitable form of mortgage for a client but does include making arrangements for, or giving advice on, any life insurance with an investment element.

Generally, investment business which is incidental to legal business does not constitute discrete investment business (DIB), ie. mainstream investment business, and is not subject to most of the rules applicable to investment business. However, this exception does not apply to *life policies* and *unit trusts* and advice on an endowment policy which is incidental to a conveyancing transaction therefore still amounts to discrete investment business.

The majority of solicitors who are authorised to give investment advice are authorised via the Law Society which is a Recognised Professional Body (RPB) under the Act. Solicitors who are granted an investment business certificate by the Society are required to comply with the Solicitors' Investment Business Rules 1990. These rules are very detailed and extremely complex. Consequently, unless a firm is of substantial size and has its own specialist investment department, it is unusual for it to engage directly in investment business. Instead many firms act through an organisation called The Solicitors' Financial Services Company. This company was established under the auspices of the Law Society to provide independent financial advice. The requirements imposed on firms are then more limited as the solicitor is using a permitted third party and the financial advice is actually being given by the company.

4.5.1 Disclosing commission

Rule 10 of the Solicitors' Practice Rules 1988 provides that solicitors shall account for any commission received of more than £20 unless, having disclosed to the client in writing the amount or basis of calculation of the commission or an approximation thereof, they have the client's agreement to retain it.

Note

Commissions on arranging life insurance policies are substantial.

Capital Gains Tax relief 4.6

One area of taxation on which sellers or buyers may require advice is Capital Gains Tax (CGT). A disposal of an interest in land for more than its acquisition cost will *prima facie* constitute a chargeable gain subject to CGT.

There is one particular relief from Capital Gains Tax which is of great importance in domestic conveyancing – ss.222–226, Taxation of Chargeable Gains Act 1992.

Sections 222–226 provide that a gain accruing to an individual on the disposal of a dwelling-house or part of a dwelling-house including grounds of up to 0.5 of a hectare shall not be a chargeable gain if it has been occupied as the individual's only or main residence throughout their period of ownership. The permitted area can be larger than 0.5 hectare if the Inland Revenue Commissions are satisfied that having regard to the size and character of the dwelling-house a larger area is required for the reasonable enjoyment of it.

A disposal of part of the grounds of the dwelling-house up to the permitted area will be exempt provided that the grounds are disposed of before the dwelling-house itself.

Where an individual has two or more residences they can elect which is to be regarded as their main residence by giving notice to the Inspector of Taxes. There are certain time limits for giving this notice. In the absence of election the question shall be concluded by the determination of the Inspector although the taxpayer has a right of appeal against the determination.

Note

Spouses living together can have only one main residence for both.

Where the taxpayer has not occupied the house throughout their period of ownership then a fraction of the gain will be chargeable. In calculating the fraction of time during which the house is to be regarded as the taxpayer's main residence, the following periods of absence from the property will be disregarded and will be treated as if the taxpayer were in occupation:

- Periods before 31 March 1982;
- The last three years of ownership;
- Periods of absence not exceeding three years;
- Periods of absence in employment overseas;
- Periods of absence not exceeding four years in which the taxpayer was required to reside elsewhere by reason of the demands of their work;
- The first 12 months' ownership (this is an extra-statutory concession).

These periods are *cumulative* so that there could in fact be a period of many years during which the taxpayer did not occupy the property and yet their absences would be disregarded and they would still be entitled to full relief.

If any part of the property has been used *exclusively for business purposes* only a part of the gain will be exempt. The proportion which will be taxable will depend on the area used for business relative to the size of the house and on the period of business user relative to the total period of ownership.

Note

The exemption will not be lost if room(s) are used for business but other members of the family also use them.

If the property does not qualify for Principal Private Residence Relief (eg. a second home) or where part of the exemption has been lost (eg. by business user) then it will be necessary to calculate the gain.

In calculating any chargeable gain you deduct from the consideration received for the disposal of the asset the acquisition cost, or if the property was acquired prior to 31 March 1982 its value at that date. The taxpayer will be entitled to offset against the gain the acquisition and disposal costs and any expenditure incurred in enhancing the value of the property: s.38, TCGA 1992. These deductions will be indexed in accordance with s.53 to take account of rises in the retail price index.

In respect of any chargeable gain the taxpayer will be entitled to an annual exemption. In the case of married couples each spouse is entitled to the annual exemption.

Self-assessment questions

1 You are acting for a client who is buying a house for £62,000 to include all carpets, curtains, cooker, fridge,

freezer, dishwasher and washing machine. What particular matter should you consider?

2 What is MIRAS? Who can claim it and how much is it worth?

3 What is the difference between a repayment mortgage and an endowment mortgage?

4 Your client owns a London house and a country cottage which she originally used as a holiday home. Five years ago she retired and moved permanently to the country but did not sell the house as her adult children were still occupying it. They have now left and she is selling. Will she be liable to Capital Gains Tax and, if so, how will it be calculated?

Chapter 5

Professional conduct

Introduction 5.1

Throughout the conveyancing transaction you must at all times observe the Solicitors' Practice Rules and the other rules, codes, written standards and guidelines issued by the Law Society. Many issues of professional practice arise at the very outset of the transaction when taking instructions to act.

Note

You should refer to The Law Society's *Guide to the Professional Conduct of Solicitors*.

Rule 15: Solicitors' Practice Rules – Client care 5.2

Rule 15 (Client Care)

1 Every principal in private practice shall operate a complaints handling procedure which shall, *inter alia*, ensure that clients are informed whom to approach in the event of any problem with the service provided.

2 Every solicitor in private practice shall, unless it is inappropriate in the circumstances:

(a) ensure that clients know the name and status of the person responsible for the day to day conduct of the matter and the principal responsible for its overall supervision;

(b) ensure that clients know whom to approach in the event of any problem with the service provided; and

(c) ensure that clients are at all relevant times given any appropriate information as to the issues raised and the progress of the matter.

After taking instructions you will write to the client to confirm your instructions and the costs quoted. In that letter you must ensure that you comply with Rule 15(2).

Note

The Law Society has issued a good practice guide on client care which gives practical advice on compliance with Rule 15 and also with the written professional standards on costs.

Costs 5.3

Information on costs 5.3.1

The Law Society has issued a set of written professional

standards concerning information on costs. It provides that:

- On taking instructions you should give the client the best information possible about the likely cost of the matter and discuss with them how the charges and disbursements are to be met;
- When confirming instructions in writing you should record whether any fee has been agreed and, if so, what it is, what it covers and whether it includes VAT and disbursements;
- The final amount payable should not vary substantially from the estimate unless clients have been informed of changed circumstances in writing.

In conveyancing solicitors do not normally charge an hourly rate but give the client a price for the job.

Note

Many conveyancing transactions do not proceed to completion. You should make it clear at the outset whether or not you will charge for uncompleted (abortive) transactions and the basis on which the charge will be made.

5.3.2 Exceeding the estimate

The price quoted may be an estimate or a fixed quote.

You should be careful to ensure that you do not bind yourself to a fixed fee, unless that is your intention, as a fixed fee cannot be increased if the transaction turns out to be more complex than you anticipated.

In the case of an estimate you should inform your client immediately it appears that the estimate will be or is likely to be exceeded; you should not wait until you submit the bill of costs.

5.3.3 Rendering the bill

You are under a duty to render a bill of costs to your client within a *reasonable time of concluding the matter* to which the bill relates.

It is good practice to submit it as soon as possible, especially where you are holding sums of money on behalf of your client and await their approval of the costs before accounting to the client for the balance. This is a common situation in conveyancing as you will often be holding sale proceeds for your client.

You may *not* transfer the costs from client account to office account unless the client has previously agreed the amount and it has in writing been made clear to the client that money held for them is being or will be applied towards such costs.

You must not sue, or threaten to sue, without first informing your client in writing of their right to require a remuneration certificate and/or to seek taxation of your bill. In any event, you may not sue your client until the expiration of one month from the delivery of your bill.

Acting for more than one party 5.4

General rule 5.4.1

There is a general principle of professional conduct that a singloe solicitor or firm should not accept instructions to act for two or more clients where there is a conflict, or a significant risk of a conflict, between the interests of those clients.

Rule 6: Solicitors' Practice Rules 5.4.2

In conveyancing the chance of there being a conflict of interest is high and therefore Rule 6 deals specifically with this issue.

Rule 6 (Prohibition against acting for seller and buyer, or for lender and borrower in a private mortgage)

1 Without prejudice to the general principle of professional conduct that a solicitor shall not accept instructions to act for two or more clients where there is a conflict between the interests of those clients, a solicitor or two or more solicitors practising in partnership or association shall not act for both seller and buyer on a transfer of land for value at arm's length, or for both lessor and lessee on the grant of a lease for value at arm's length, or for both lender and borrower in a private mortgage at arm's length.

2 Provided no conflict of interest appears, and provided the seller or lessor is not a builder or developer selling or leasing as such, and provided the solicitor or any solicitor practising in partnership or association with that solicitor is not instructed to negotiate the sale of the property concerned, the rule set out in paragraph 1 of this rule shall not apply if:

(a) the parties are associated companies; or

(b) the parties are related by blood, adoption or marriage; or

(c) both parties are established clients (which expression shall include persons related by blood, adoption or marriage to established clients); or

(d) on a transfer of land, the consideration is less than £5,000; or

(e) there is no other solicitor or other qualified conveyancer in the vicinity whom either party can reasonably be expected to consult; or

(f) two associated firms or two offices of the same firm are respectively acting for the parties, provided that:

(i) the respective firms or offices are in different localities; and

(ii) neither party was referred to the firm or office acting for him or her from an associated firm or from another office of the same firm; and

(iii) the transaction is dealt with or supervised by a different solicitor in regular attendance at each firm or office.

3 In this rule:

(a) 'association' refers to a situation where two or more firms of solicitors have at least one common principal; and where either firm is a recognised body 'principal' means a director or member of that body, or the beneficial owner of any share in the body held by a member as nominee, or the body itself; and

(b) 'private mortgage' means any mortgage other than one provided by an institution which provides mortgages in the normal course of its activities.

Note

1 The ban on acting for both parties imposed by Rule 6(1) applies even if there is no conflict of interest. The exceptions provided for in Rule 6(2) only apply if there is *no* conflict of interest.

2 A transaction is a transaction 'at arm's length' when it is intended to be a proper commercial transaction at full market value.

3 The test of whether someone is an 'established client' is an objective one, ie. whether the ordinary, reasonable and fair minded solicitor would regard a person as an established client. An *existing* client is not the same as an *established* client.

5.4.3 Acting for seller and buyer

Conflict of interest

A conflict of interest between seller and buyer may arise over any issue, eg. over the amount of the deposit or over the date for completion. The potential for a conflict arising is so great that extreme caution must be exercised before you accept instructions to act for both. The consent of both clients to the arrangement must always be obtained.

If at any time during the course of a transaction where you may properly act for both parties a conflict arises between them, you must *not continue* to act for both. You may continue to act for one of them provided you are not in possession of confidential information obtained while acting for the other. The consent of the other client must be sought and, in the absence of consent, you should only continue to act for the one if the withholding of consent is unreasonable. Generally, you will continue to act for the more established client.

Undue influence

One particular situation in which you should never act for both, even if one of the Rule 6(2) exceptions applies, is where there is a possibility that one party may exercise *undue influence* over the other (*see* Chapter 18, para. 18.4.2). If there is any possibility of undue influence later being alleged it is vital that the parties are separately represented. This applies not only between seller and buyer, lessor and lessee and mortgagor and mortgagee, but also between co-buyers and co-mortgagors.

Acting for more than one buyer 5.4.4

If there is more than one buyer then there could be a conflict of interest as to how the beneficial title is to be held; whether as *joint tenants* or *tenants in common*.

The two forms of co-ownership will have to be carefully explained to the buyers and their wishes ascertained. They will probably ask for your advice. The generally accepted view is that in the case of a married couple a beneficial joint tenancy may be appropriate but that in other situations, a tenancy in common is probably preferable.

There may also be a conflict of interest as to the shares in which tenants in common should hold, especially if the parties are contributing unequally. You must then address the question of whether they should hold in shares which reflect their respective interests.

If there is any hint of disagreement between them, or of undue influence being exercised by one over the other, then you must ensure that they are separately advised on this specific issue. This does not mean that you cannot continue to act for both in connection with the purchase, just that they must be separately advised on the issue of their beneficial holding.

Acting for the seller's mortgagee 5.4.5

Where the seller has a mortgage on the property they are selling, it will have to be redeemed at completion; usually out of the proceeds of sale. The seller's solicitor will write to the mortgagee asking for the title deeds and will undertake to hold them on behalf of the mortgagee pending sale and on sale to redeem the mortgage (*see* 5.8.1). In this situation you are not retained by and are not acting for the mortgagee but you are bound by the terms of your undertaking.

Note

The Rule 6(1) ban on acting for both a mortgagor and a private mortgagee only applies when a mortgage is being created and does not apply to this situation.

Sometimes the mortgagee will insist on being separately represented, eg. by a firm that always acts for them. In such a case completion is likely to be at the office of the mortgagee's solicitor rather than at the office of the seller's solicitor as normally occurs.

Note

Some building societies will not release the title documents to sole practitioners. Similarly, on a purchase many building societies will not instruct sole practitioners.

5.4.6 Acting for the buyer's mortgagee

In the majority of transactions the buyer buys with the aid of a mortgage. It is quite usual for the same solicitor to act for the buyer and for the buyer's mortgagee, provided that the mortgagee is an institutional lender, eg. a bank or building society and not a private individual and provided there is no conflict of interest.

Acting for both is acceptable as:

- An institutional lender will have their own mortgage deeds which cannot generally be modified. The solicitor will have to explain to the buyer the terms of the mortgage but will not have to negotiate or draft the terms of the mortgage.
- Both the buyer and their mortgagee are concerned to ensure that the buyer obtains a good title from the seller and that therefore the title is a good security for the mortgagee to lend against.

5.5 Property fraud

The Law Society has issued a warning to solicitors to be vigilant to protect their clients and themselves against fraud. It has suggested signs to watch for, eg. misrepresentation of the purchase price or unusual instructions, and steps to be taken to minimise fraud, eg. verifying the identity and *bona fides* of a client or solicitors' firm not known to you and verifying signatures.

Note

A failure to observe these signs and/or take the appropriate steps may constitute negligence.

Mortgagees' instructions 5.5.1

An increased awareness of the risks of mortgage fraud coupled with the fall in the property market which resulted in many mortgage debts being inadequately secured (negative equity) has resulted in mortgagees increasing the requirements imposed on solicitors acting for them. While some solicitors take the view that these instructions require no more of the mortgagee's solicitor than should have been done anyway, others regard them as unreasonable, particularly when they require the solicitor to confirm that the valuation of the property by the mortgagee's surveyor is based on correct information.

This had led to a debate as to whether buyers and their mortgagees should be separately represented. This would increase buyers' costs and it is doubtful whether it would relieve the buyer's solicitor of the burden of the mortgagee's requirements. Current practice, wherever mortgagees are separately represented, is for the mortgagee's solicitor to require the buyer's solicitor to provide answers to all their queries and to confirm that the title is good.

Solicitors' liability 5.5.2

It is clear that solicitors need to be extremely cautious whenever mortgage finance is involved, even where they are not instructed by the mortgagee. There have been a number of recent cases in which mortgagees have been able to recover from solicitors losses sustained through mortgage fraud and also through the overvaluation of property and the fall in the property market.

Example

In *Mortgage Express Ltd v Bowerman* (1995) a solicitor was held liable in negligence for failing to alert the mortgagee for whom they were acting to the fact that the purchaser was a sub-purchaser and that the price and the mortgage valuation were considerably higher than the price being paid for the property by the seller. As the claim was in tort rather than for breach of contract, the solicitor was liable, on restitutionary principles, not just for the difference between the mortgage valuation and the actual value of the property, but for the whole of the loss sustained by the mortgagee, including, therefore, the loss incurred by the fall in the market.

In *Penn v Bristol & West Building Society* (1995) a seller's solicitor was held liable to the buyer's mortgagee for breach of warranty of authority by impliedly representing that they had the authority of both the sellers when in fact they had not seen the wife and the husband had forged his wife's signature. The particularly worrying aspect of this type of action is that the liability is not dependant on the solicitor having been negligent.

5.6 Money laundering

Money laundering is where the identity of 'dirty money' (the proceeds of crime) is changed so that it appears to originate from a legitimate source. It is criminal offence to:

- Assist in money laundering;
- Tip off anyone of whom the authorities are suspicious;
- Fail to report someone whom you know or suspect may be involved in money laundering.

Conveyancers handle large sums of client money and must always be alert to the possibility that the source of finance may be criminal.

Solicitors who engage in investment business, whether discrete of non-discrete, must also comply with the Money Laundering Regulations 1993. These regulations give affect to an EC Directive on the prevention of the use of the financial system for the purpose of money laundering. They require firms to maintain certain procedures to forestall or prevent money laundering, and to keep records so that those investigating money laundering do not lose 'the audit trail'.

5.7 Contract races

A contract race occurs when a seller's solicitor is instructed to deal with more than one prospective buyer at the same time.

5.7.1 The Law Society Rule

Rule 6A of the *Solicitors' Practice Rules* provides that where a seller instructs a solicitor to deal with more than one prospective buyer, the solicitor (with the client's consent) shall immediately disclose the seller's decision, if possible by telephone or fax, to the solicitor or other conveyancer acting for each prospective buyer or direct to the prospective buyer if acting in person. Such disclosure, if made by telephone, shall at once be confirmed by letter or fax. Each prospective buyer must be notified each time a decision is taken to deal with any further prospective buyer.

Note

What must be notified is the seller's decision to deal with more than one prospective buyer. You must not wait until contracts are actually submitted before notifying the appropriate parties. You will have been instructed to deal with a prospective buyer where you are asked to submit a draft contract or provide any other documentation or information in order to facilitate the conveyancing of the premises

The obligations set out in the Rule also apply when the client to your knowledge deals directly or through another solicitor or conveyancer with another buyer.

A solicitor shall not act for more than one of the prospective buyers nor for the seller and one of the prospective buyers, even in a case which would fall within Rule 6(2) (*see* 5.4.2).

The perils of contract races 5.7.2

Although a contract race may at first appear attractive to a seller who has more than one interested buyer it does have its dangers. In particular, buyers may not be prepared to participate in a race and thereby risk their time and money in surveys and legal costs. All the buyers may withdraw.

It is important that the terms of the race are clear to all parties. It may be a 'first past the post' race, ie. as soon as a buyer is ready to exchange the seller must exchange with that buyer. If so the seller must make sure that they impose a deadline on the exchange of contracts otherwise their offer to exchange with whichever buyer is ready first may have to remain open indefinitely until a buyer is eventually ready to exchange.

A 'first past the post' race is not appropriate if the seller has a related purchase which they need to synchronise with the sale. The terms of the race should then be that, if and when the seller is ready to exchange, they will do so with the buyer who was ready first.

Gazumping 5.7.3

Gazumping occurs when a seller has accepted an offer from one buyer – but contracts have not yet been exchanged and the parties are therefore not yet legally bound – and then accepts a higher offer from another buyer. Sometimes this will result in the draft contract that was submitted to the first buyer being withdrawn; sometimes it will result in a contract race. There are no special rules applicable to gazumping. Provided the direction on contract races is followed, it is not unprofessional to act for a seller who seeks to secure a higher price.

Note

The fact that gazumping is possible clearly demonstrates that there is no legally binding contract until contracts are exchanged.

5.8 Undertakings

For the effect of undertakings generally you are referred to the Law Society's *Guide to the Professional Conduct of Solicitors*.

Remember:

- A solicitor who fails to honour an undertaking is *prima facie* guilty of professional misconduct;
- An undertaking is still binding even if it is to do something outside the solicitor's control (therefore never undertake to do anything you may not be able to do);
- Before undertaking to deal with the client's money in a particular way you must have the client's authority to do so.

In conveyancing, undertakings are extensively used at various stages of the transaction.

5.8.1 Obtaining title documents from the seller's mortgagee

When acting for a seller whose property is mortgaged you must obtain the charge certificate (or title deeds in the case of an unregistered title) from the mortgagee. Immediately after receiving instructions to act you will therefore write to the mortgagee requesting the charge certificate/title deeds for the purpose of sale. In that letter you will undertake to hold the documents to the order of the mortgagee and to return them to the mortgagee on demand pending completion of the transaction. If the transaction is completed you will be bound to pay to the mortgagee the amount of the mortgage money and you must therefore be certain that the proceeds of sale will be sufficient to discharge the mortgage.

Note

Bank mortgagees often require more extensive undertakings in which they are promised the whole of the sale proceeds less estate agent's commission and legal costs and disbursements, and they will generally not permit any variation of the terms of their standard undertakings.

5.8.2 Bridging finance

This is short term borrowing to bridge (cover) a period of

time before certain other funds become available. It is readily provided by banks if they can see a source from which the borrowing will be repaid in the not too distant future. It is, however, expensive both in terms of the interest rate and the bank's arrangement fee. It is therefore to be avoided if at all possible.

It may, however, be necessary to raise bridging finance at various stages of the transaction.

The deposit

The buyer may be funding the purchase entirely from the proceeds of sale of an existing property and/or a mortgage on the new property. Neither of these sources of finance will be available until completion. However, at exchange of contracts a 10% deposit will normally have to be paid and funding this may be a problem. It may be possible to persuade the seller to agree to a smaller deposit and where an existing property is being sold it will usually be possible to use the deposit received on that sale towards the deposit on the related purchase. Sometimes, however, it will be necessary to raise bridging finance for all or part of the deposit.

The completion money

If there is a delay on a buyer's related sale or on the arrival of the mortgage funds then the buyer will not have the money to complete. They will either have to delay their purchase, which will involve them in liability to the seller, or they will have to raise bridging finance in order to complete.

The solicitor's undertaking

When a client obtains bridging finance the bank will require an undertaking from the client's solicitor with respect to the repayment of the loan. The undertaking will, for example, promise that the loan will be repaid by paying over to the bank the proceeds of a related sale less certain specified deductions. There are certain forms of undertaking which have been agreed between the Law Society and the clearing banks.

Undertaking for discharge of seller's mortgage 5.8.3

A seller with a mortgage on the property they are selling will generally need to obtain the proceeds of sale before they can pay off the mortgage. If they are required to pay it off before completion, and therefore before their sale proceeds are available, they may have to raise bridging finance to do so. Buyers are generally reasonable about this and do not insist on the seller discharging the mortgage pre-completion but permit them to do so post-completion out of the proceeds of sale.

The buyer's solicitor will agree to this because of the strength of solicitors' undertakings. The seller's solicitor will undertake to forward the money necessary to redeem the mortgage to the mortgagee and then, when they receive from the mortgagee the proof of discharge (which will be a Form 53 if the title is registered and a receipt endorsed on the mortgage deed where it is unregistered), to forward it to the buyer's solicitor.

Note

The seller's solicitor does not undertake that the Form 53/ receipt will be issued by the mortgagee as this is not within the solicitor's control.

The Law Society has approved the following form of words for use in relation to building society mortgages:

In consideration of your today completing the purchaser of ... WE HEREBY UNDERTAKE forthwith to pay over to the ... Building Society the money required to redeem the mortgage/legal charge dated ... and to forward the receipted mortgage/legal charge to you as soon as it is received by us from the ... Building Society.

A similar undertaking will be accepted where the mortgagee is an established bank but in the case of a private mortgage the buyer's solicitor should not complete on the basis of an undertaking but should insist on the mortgage being discharged pre-completion and the evidence of discharge handed over at completion (*see* Chapter 11, para. 11.3.3). This is because there is a risk that a private mortgagee may fail to issue the Form 53/receipt.

Note

The vast majority of domestic conveyancing transactions involve the discharge of a seller's mortgage and completion on the basis of the seller's solicitor giving an undertaking with regard to the discharge of the mortgage. This undertaking is a vital mechanism for the smooth functioning of the conveyancing process.

5.8.4 Miscellaneous undertakings

There are many other situations in which undertakings are used, for example they are:

- Embodied in the Law Society formulae for exchange of contracts (*see* Chapter 10, para. 10.2.3).
- Embodied in the Law Society Code for Completion by Post (*see* Chapter 12, para. 12.4.1).
- Given by the seller's solicitor to assist with any requisitions (queries) which the Land Registry may raise on an

application for first registration of title (*see* Chapter 17, para. 17.2.3).

Client account rules 5.9

Conveyancers handle very large sums of money. The Solicitors' Accounts Rules 1991 must be scrupulously applied at all times.

The following must all be paid into client account and separate ledger entries must be maintained for each client:

1 Proceeds of sale;

2 Mortgage advance cheques;

3 Funds supplied by the client;

4 Deposit received on a client's sale including a deposit received on a stakeholder basis (*see* Chapter 8, para. 8.7.1).

The client's money can only be used on the client's authority for:

1 Payment of the deposit on their purchase;

2 Payment of the balance of the price;

3 Fees of third parties, eg. estate agents, counsel;

4 Stamp duty and Land Registry fees;

5 Costs, including VAT, and disbursements such as search fees (*see* 5.3.3).

Note

Items 3 and 4 must be paid directly from client account and the amounts must not be moved to office account prior to the payment of these items.

Client money must *never* be used for:

- Other client's transactions;
- The firm's expenses.

Interest on client account 5.9.1

Money held in client account will earn interest and a solicitor must account to the client for that interest in accordance with the following table.

No of weeks held	*Minimum amount held (£)*
8	1,000
4	2,000
2	10,000
1	20,000

Where the solicitor holds a sum of money exceeding £20,000 for less than a week they shall account to the client for the interest if it is fair and reasonable to do so having regard to all the circumstances.

In conveyancing very large sums are frequently held but usually only for a couple of days. In such cases the cost of working out the interest earned and making the payment may well outweigh the amount involved and if the amount involved is less than £20 the solicitor will not be expected to account for it.

In the case of money held as a stakeholder the solicitor shall pay interest in accordance with the above rules to the person to whom the stake is eventually paid, ie. if completion takes place it will be payable to the seller.

Nothing in the Accounts Rules shall affect any arrangement in writing made between a solicitor and client as to the application of the client's money or interest thereon, including interest on stakeholder money.

On the face of it, this seems to entitle a solicitor to contract out of the interest provisions. However the Law Society has issued a guidance note which demonstrates that caution should be exercised and that it is considered improper for a solicitor to request a client to enter into an arrangement in writing with a view to paying no interest at all. A stipulation for a £20 *de minimis* exception would nevertheless be acceptable.

So far as money held as stakeholder is concerned it may be acceptable to include a special provision in the contract that the solicitor stakeholder retains the interest on the deposit to cover their charges for acting as stakeholder. The guidance note states that this is only acceptable if it will provide fair and reasonable remuneration for the work and risk involved in holding a stake.

5.10 Miscellaneous

The conveyancing transaction may give rise to many other issues of professional conduct which are subject to specific Law Society rules. Full consideration of all of these is beyond the scope of this companion but they are covered in The Law Society's *Guide to the Professional Conduct of Solicitors.*

- Council Statement on Dealing with Licensed Conveyancers (1987);
- Council Statement on Dealing with Unqualified Conveyancers (1988, revised 1990);
- Council Statement on Property Selling by Solicitors (1990);

- Council Statement on the Financial Services Act 1986: Life Policies and Tied Agents (1988, revised 1990);
- Solicitors' Investment Business Rules (1990);
- Receipt of Commissions from Third Parties (Rule 10 Solicitors' Practice Rules 1991).

Self-assessment questions

1 In what circumstances may the same solicitor or firm of solicitors act for both seller and buyer?

2 Where there is more than one buyer interested in the property the seller may institute a contract rate. What are the advantages and disadvantages of this for (a) the seller and (b) the buyer?

3 Explain why solicitors' undertakings are so valuable and give three examples of their use in conveyancing.

4 When can you take out of client account:

(a) Your costs

(b) The money to pay the stamp duty to the Inland Revenue

(c) The money required to repay a bridging loan taken out by the client?

Chapter 6

Physical aspects

Surveys 6.1

The seller does not owe any duty to the buyer to disclose physical defects in the property. The maxim *caveat emptor* (let the buyer beware) applies, so the buyer must ensure that they check the physical state of the property.

When the buyer is buying with the aid of a mortgage the prospective mortgagee will do a survey in order to decide whether the value of the property constitutes sufficient security for the loan which is being granted. The mortgagee will require the survey fee from the prospective buyer before they institute the survey.

Mortgagees generally offer buyers a choice between a simple *valuation survey* and a somewhat more detailed (and more expensive) *home buyer's survey*. However, neither of these is a full structural survey and they may not reveal all defects in the property, eg. on a mortgage survey the surveyor will probably not go into the loft or remove carpets to examine the floorboards.

The age and nature of the property will largely determine whether or not a full structural survey is advisable. For example, buying an eighteenth-century country house is a very different proposition from buying a 1980s 'semi' and a full survey will probably be advisable in the former case but not necessarily in the latter. A full structural survey is, however, very expensive.

Note

You should explain to your client the different types of survey available but the decision as to which type to have must be the client's.

Surveyor's liability 6.1.1

Where the buyer commissions their own survey, the surveyor is under a contractual duty to them to carry out the survey with the requisite degree of care and skill. If the survey fails to reveal certain defects in the property then the surveyor may possibly be liable for breach of contract. If the contract with the surveyor contains exclusion clauses then the reasonableness of those clauses under the Unfair Contract Terms Act 1977 will have to be considered.

In the case of the mortgagee's survey there is no contractual relationship between the buyer and the surveyor. However, in *Smith v Eric S Bush* (1990) the House of Lords held that 'the valuer who values a house for the purpose of a mortgage, knowing that the mortgagee will rely and the mortgagor will probably rely on the valuation, knowing that the purchaser mortgagor has in effect paid for the valuation, is under a duty to exercise reasonable skill and care and that duty is owed to both parties to the mortgage for which the valuation is made'.

The House of Lords also considered whether a disclaimer of liability was reasonable under s.2, Unfair Contract Terms Act 1977. In concluding that the disclaimer was not reasonable, their Lordships took account of the factual circumstances in which domestic valuations for mortgage purposes are conducted and the fact that the valuer knows that 90% of purchasers rely on the mortgage valuation and do not commission their own survey. The fact that the valuer knows full well that failure on their part to exercise reasonable skill and care may be disastrous to the purchaser may also have influenced the Law Lords' decision. They made it clear that their decision was:

> in respect of a dwelling-house of modest value in which it is widely recognised by surveyors that purchasers are in fact relying on their care and skills;

but reserved their position:

> in respect of valuations of quite different types of property for mortgage purposes such as industrial property, large blocks of flats or very expensive houses. In such cases it may well be that the general expectation of behaviour of the purchaser is quite different. With very large sums of money at stake prudence would seem to demand that the purchaser obtains his own structural survey to guide him in his purchase and in such circumstances with very much larger sums of money at stake it may be reasonable for the surveyors valuing on behalf of those who are providing the finance, either to exclude or limit their liability to the purchaser.

6.2 NHBC

The National House-Building Council is an organisation of house builders and developers. It sets minimum standards of construction, inspects properties as they are built to ensure compliance with those standards and operates a scheme known as Buildmark which provides protection for buyers of new houses for up to 10 years after construction. Over 90% of new homes are constructed by builders who are members of NHBC. Those who are not will find that they probably need to take out similar forms of insurance cover in order to make their properties marketable. There are a number of commercial insurers who provide cover similar to that provided under the Buildmark Scheme.

Under the Buildmark Scheme a buyer's protection falls into three phases.

- Up to the completion of the construction of the property: during this period the buyer is protected against the risk of the builder going into liquidation and failing to complete the construction. They will be covered for any loss of deposit or for the cost of completing the property to NHBC standards.
- For two years following the completion of the construction and the issue of the 10 year notice of cover. This is known as the *initial guarantee period*. If during this period faults appear in the property then the buyer must contact the builder to rectify them but if the builder has gone into liquidation or otherwise fails to carry out the necessary repairs, then the buyer can claim on the insurance policy that backs the guarantee.
- From two to 10 years after construction. This is known as the *structural guarantee period*. The buyer is only protected in respect of major damage caused by *structural faults* in the property or by *subsidence or heave*. During this period there is no obligation on the buyer to first seek out the builder and try and get him to rectify the fault, the buyer can immediately make a claim on the NHBC insurance cover.

Thus, under the NHBC Buildmark Scheme there are varying degrees of insurance cover in respect of the physical state of the property for up to 10 years after its construction. If the first buyer sells the property before 10 years then the benefit of the Buildmark cover will be transferred to the next buyer and so on.

Note

Where mortgage finance is being raised in order to buy a newly-constructed property or one constructed within the last 10 years, it will be a normal condition of the mortgage offer that there is NHBC cover. If this does not exist the mortgagee will have to be notified and may require some alternative commercial structural guarantee insurance to be effected.

Planning 6.3

Town and country planning is regulated by the Town and Country Planning Act 1990 and the Planning and Compensation Act 1991. Planning is the responsibility of the local planning authority, ie. the local council.

The local planning authority must produce plans setting out their policy for the area for which they are responsible. In metropolitan areas including London these are known as unitary development plans, whereas in non-metropolitan areas there are structure and local plans. Structure plans are prepared by the county council and approved by the Secretary of State for the Environment and local plans are prepared by district planning authorities. All these plans are written statements of the authorities' policy and proposals for the area for which they are responsible.

In the non-metropolitan areas where there are the two tiers of planning authority, the purpose of the local plan is to develop the structure plan at a more detailed level but it must fall within the general policy framework of the structure plan.

These plans will give you an indication as to whether you are likely to obtain planning permission for a particular type of development in a particular area.

6.3.1 Development

Planning permission is needed for anything that constitutes development. Development means 'the carrying out of building, engineering, mining or other operations in, on, and over or under land, or the making of any material change in the use of any buildings or other land': s.55, Town and Country Planning Act 1990.

Development therefore has two aspects to it:

- The *operational* aspect, and
- The *change of user* aspect.

The following activities do *not* involve development.

1 The carrying out for the maintenance, improvement or other alteration of any building of *works* which affect only the *interior* of the building or do not materially affect the *external appearance* of the building.

Note

If the building is of special historic or architectural interest there are special controls under the Planning (Listed Buildings and Conservation Areas) Act 1990 and even minor interior alterations will require special permission.

2 The *use* of any building or other land within the curtilage of a dwelling-house for any *purpose incidental to the enjoyment* of the dwelling-house as such.

There is no hard and fast definition of *curtilage*. It is defined in the Oxford English Dictionary as 'a small court, yard, garth, or piece of ground attached to a dwelling-house and forming one enclosure with it, or so regarded by the law; the area attached to and containing a dwelling-house and its outbuildings'.

Since 'use' does not include building operations this provision does not authorise the erection of sheds, greenhouses or other buildings within the curtilage, but development of this type may be permitted development under the General Development Order depending on the size and location of the building.

3 In the case of buildings or other land which are used for a purpose of any class specified in an order made by the Secretary of State, the *use* thereof for any purpose of the same class.

Note

The Act specifically provides that the use as two or more separate dwelling-houses of any building previously used as a single dwelling-house does involve a material change in use.

The Use Classes Order 6.3.2

The Town and Country Planning (Use Classes) Order 1987 provides for 16 different classes of user divided into four groups: A, B, C and D. Where someone wishes to change the user of their premises to another user within the same class under the 1987 Order that does not constitute development and therefore does not require planning permission, eg. changing within Class A1 from a toy shop to a clothes shop, changing within Class A2 from a solicitor's office to a building society.

Class A1

Class A1 includes most types of shop other than those selling hot food. It includes hairdressers, travel agencies and dry cleaners.

Class A2

Class A2 covers financial and professional services which it is appropriate to provide in a shopping area where the services are provided principally to visiting members of the public.

Class A3

Class A3 covers premises selling food and drink for consumption on the premises or of hot food for consumption off the premises.

Class B1

Class B1 covers use as an office other than a use within Class A2, and the use of premises for research and development of products or processes or for any industrial process which can be carried on in a residential area without detriment to the amenity of the area.

Class B2

Class B2 comprises general industrial user and there are further classes under Part B dealing with other special industrial groups.

Note

Although a change of user within the same class does not involve development and therefore does not require planning permission, if building operations are also involved then planning permission may be required for the building work.

6.3.3 The General Development Order

Planning permission is required for anything that constitutes development: s.57, Town and Country Planning Act 1990. However, you do not always have to apply for a specific permission because it may be development which is permitted under the Town and Country Planning (General Development) Order 1988 (GDO). This provides a ready-made permission for development in a number of specified classes.

Class 1

Class 1 permits development within the curtilage of a dwelling-house so long as certain restrictions are observed, ie. as to the height and size of the extended building. Erecting a garage is sometimes treated as an enlargement of the house depending on the proximity of the garage to the house. Adding a porch to the front of the house may similarly come within this permitted development. Many ordinary domestic extensions fall within this class of permitted development.

Class 2

Under Class 2 many minor operations such as erecting fences, gates, walls etc. or painting the exterior of the property are permitted, but again the restrictions imposed by the GDO must be observed, eg. as to the height of fences, particularly those that abut the highway.

6.3.4 Article 4 directions

The local planning authority may direct that all or any of the permissions granted by the GDO shall not apply to the whole or part of the area for which it is responsible. The pre-contract enquiries of the local authority will reveal whether there is an Article 4 direction in force affecting the area in which the property is situated. For example, a local authority may decide that in relation to a particular area, eg. a new estate, it does not want everyone to have the benefit of the development permitted by the GDO but wishes even minor developments to be the subject of specific applications for planning permission.

Specific applications 6.3.5

An express application for planning permission must be made for any development that does not come within the development authorised by the GDO. Where the permission being sought is permission to erect a building the initial application does not need to be a detailed one but can be an application for outline permission only. This means a planning permission which is granted subject to the reservation for subsequent approval by the local planning authority or the Secretary of State of certain reserved matters. For example, permission may be granted for the construction of a new block of flats of a certain size and height but the detail of what the block will look like so far as the type of brick, roof tiles, windows etc. to be used may be the subject of a reservation: s.92, Town and Country Planning Act 1990.

Note

If you are not sure whether your proposals constitute development and therefore require planning permission and, if so, whether or not they fall within the GDO, you can apply to the local authority for a determination on these preliminary issues.

The local planning authority must keep a register of all planning applications and of the authority's decisions on those applications. The register is open to public inspection. The pre-contract enquiries of the local authority will reveal where the register is kept and its opening hours. Where planning permission is granted it is not generally personal to the applicant but attaches to the land so that the land carries with it the benefit of the planning permission. In some circumstances this may greatly enhance the value of the land.

When granting permission the local planning authority may impose such conditions as it think fits: s.70, Town and Country Planning Act 1990. Such conditions constitute local land charges.

Duration of planning permission 6.3.6

An ordinary planning permission lasts for five years so the

development must be commenced within that time. An outline planning permission is subject to conditions that:

- The application for approval of reserved matters is made within three years; and
- Development must be begun within five years of the grant of the outlined permission or within two years of the approval of reserved matters whichever is the later: s.92, Town and Country Planning Act 1990.

6.3.7 Enforcement of planning legislation

Carrying out development without the required planning permission or failing to comply with any condition or limitation subject to which planning permission has been granted constitutes a breach of planning control.

Where it appears to the local planning authority that there has been a breach of planning control, the local planning authority may issue an enforcement notice: s.172, Town and Country Planning Act 1990.

An enforcement notice requires the breach to be remedied, eg. it requires the condition attached to the consent to be complied with or requires the discontinuance of an unauthorised user or the removal of an unauthorised building.

There are time limits within which the local authority must issue an enforcement notice if it is going to do so. The time limit is four years where the breach consists of the carrying out of operations or the change of use of any building to use as a single dwelling-house. For all other breaches the time limit is 10 years: s.171B, Town and Country Planning Act 1990 (as amended by s.4, Planning and Compensation Act 1991).

Where an enforcement notice is not complied with within the compliance period, the local authority may enter the property and take for itself the steps necessary to comply with the enforcement notice. Reasonable costs for doing so can be charged to the owner of the land.

Non-compliance with an operative enforcement notice constitutes a criminal offence.

6.3.8 Building regulations

Even where planning permission is not required, compliance with the building regulations will still be necessary. These are regulations which ensure that the property is built or altered according to certain health and safety standards.

Building regulations deal with matters such as the materials to be used in the construction, the depth of the foundations and drainage and ventilation of the building. During the course of the construction/alteration, the work will be inspected, either by a local authority inspector or by some other approved inspector such as the NHBC, to ensure compliance with the building regulations.

Although the local authority only has 12 months within which to take action for any breach of the building regulations, the certificate of approval should be kept indefinitely with the title documents as a subsequent buyer will always be concerned to know that any building work, whenever carried out, complied with the regulations.

Self-assessment questions

1 What is the difference between the initial guarantee period and the structural guarantee period under the Buildmark Scheme?

2 What is the difference between the Use Classes Order and the General Development Order?

3 On behalf of a prospective buyer you have made certain pre-contract enquiries of the local authority. These have revealed that the property in question is within an area affected by an Article 4 direction. What practical effect will this have on your client?

4 What time limits apply to the:

(a) Commencement of development;

(b) Service by the local authority of an enforcement notice?

Chapter 7

Deducing and investigating title

Deducing title 7.1

The seller must deduce title to the estate being sold, ie. the seller must prove that they are capable of transferring title to the buyer.

Generally this is proved by showing that the seller is the registered proprietor. Sometimes the property is registered in someone else's name but the seller can nevertheless prove the right to sell it (*see* 7.1.3).

The seller must also provide details of incumbrances which affect the title and subject to which the property is being sold. There must be no other incumbrances on the title other than those provided for in the contract.

Method 7.1.1

Title must be deduced in accordance with s.110, LRA 1925. This requires the seller to provide the buyer with:

- A copy of the subsisting entries in the Register;
- A copy of any filed plan;
- Copies or abstracts, ie. summaries, of any documents or any part thereof noted on the Register so far as they affect the land to be dealt with;
- Subject to any contrary stipulation, copies, abstracts and evidence (if any) in respect of any subsisting rights and interests appurtenant to the registered land as to which the Register is not conclusive, and of any matters excepted from the effect of registration, eg. overriding interests.

Section 110 does not specifically require the copies of the entries in the Register, which the seller provides, to be office copies, ie. official copies issued by the Land Registry. Photocopies of the entries in the land/charge certificate would possibly satisfy s.110. However, the certificate may not reflect the current state of the Register as certain entries can be made without the production of the certificate (*see* Chapter 2, para. 2.3). Although a seller will normally provide office copies, a buyer should always ensure that the contract requires the seller to provide them so that the buyer receives proof of the current state of the Register and so that pre-completion they will be able to do a Form 94 search which can only be done as from the date of the office copies.

7.1.2 **Time**

Traditionally title is deduced after the exchange of contracts but where the title is registered the process of deducing title is straightforward and therefore it has long been the practice to deduce title pre-contract by providing office copies with the draft contract (or shortly thereafter).

Note

Where the National Conveyancing Protocol is being followed, title is always deduced pre-contract.

7.1.3 **The seller who is not the registered proprietor**

There are various situations where the seller is not the registered proprietor but is able to prove the right to dispose of the title.

Mortgagee

A mortgagee (registered chargee) whose power of sale has arisen is able to transfer the registered proprietor's (mortgagor's) title to a buyer. The buyer will need to see the mortgage deed to check that the power of sale has arisen (*see* 7.5).

Personal representatives

Where a sole or last surviving registered proprietor dies, title vests in their personal representatives (PRs) and by producing the grant of representation the PRs can be registered as the new proprietors. They can, however, dispose of the property without ever being registered.

Title will then be proved by the PRs producing office copies showing the deceased as registered proprietor and the grant of representation proving their right to deal with the deceased's estate (*see* Chapter 18, para. 18.1). The death certificate of the deceased proprietor will not be necessary.

Re-sale

A buyer may contract to re-sell to a sub-buyer and may never themselves become the registered proprietor. The seller in the re-sale contract will prove title by showing that the head seller is registered as proprietor and that the sub-seller (the first buyer) has a binding contract with the proprietor (the head seller) for the transfer of the title. There will generally then be a transfer from the head seller directly to the sub-buyer, although the intermediate buyer may also be a party to the transfer.

Note

All these situations, ie. sales by mortgagees, personal representatives and sub-sales, require the seller to produce further documents beyond those specified in s.110 in order to prove their right to deal with the title. Where the seller could have become the registered proprietor the buyer may insist that they do so, but this is rarely done. Thus, buyers do not usually insist on PRs or sub-sellers becoming registered as proprietors but are content to deal with them on proof that they could have been so registered.

Investigating title 7.2

The buyer's solicitor must:

- Check the *evidence of title* supplied by the seller to ensure that the seller can transfer title;
- Check for *third party rights* which will be binding on a buyer.

  Those which are removable or overreachable should be appropriately dealt with to ensure that the buyer will not be subject to them. Others which cannot be removed or overreached will bind the buyer and the buyer must therefore decide whether or not to proceed with the purchase.

Method 7.2.1

- Examine the office copies and other documents supplied by the seller (*see* 7.1.1). These will prove the seller's title and show the entries in the Register protecting minor interests. They should also provide such documentary evidence as exists of overriding interests.
- Make pre-contract enquiries of the seller and ensure inspection of the property to discover overriding interests, eg. legal easements and the rights of those in occupation.
- Do a local land charges search.
- Shortly before completion check, by means of a Land Registry search and a further inspection, that the position has not changed (*see* Chapter 11, para. 11.4).

Dispositions by a sole proprietor 7.3

Where the title is registered in a sole name there may be other people who have a beneficial interest in the property. You must check to see if there is any restriction or caution protecting such an interest as a minor interest and also check whether there is anyone in occupation with such an interest as this would constitute an overriding interest. If a beneficial interest is discovered you *must* ensure that it is overreached.

Whenever title is registered in a sole name there is also the danger of the existence of a MHA right. If there is a notice protecting such a right, you must ensure that it is removed by the spouse who entered it (*see* 7.6.3).

7.4 Dispositions by a surviving co-owner

7.4.1 Legal co-ownership

Up to four people can hold the legal estate and therefore be registered as proprietors of the legal title. Most cases of co-ownership involve only two co-owners, eg. husband and wife, but if there are three or four co-owners then they must *all* be party to any disposition and a disposition by two only will not be effective to transfer the legal title.

7.4.2 Death of a legal co-owner

Legal co-owners must hold as joint tenants on trust for sale. When one dies the right of survivorship automatically operates and the survivor(s) alone has legal title. The PRs of the deceased co-owner *never* acquire the legal title and therefore will not be involved in any subsequent disposition of it. Only on the death of the last surviving co-owner does the legal title pass to the deceased's PRs.

A sole surviving co-owner has sole legal title and can dispose of the legal title on their own. Whether or not the buyer should insist on the appointment of a second trustee will depend on how the beneficial title was held.

7.4.3 Beneficial joint tenants

Where co-owners are holding on trust for sale for themselves as beneficial joint tenants, the right of survivorship will operate as regards both the legal and the beneficial title.

A sole surviving co-owner will therefore have both sole legal and sole beneficial title and a buyer can safely deal with the survivor alone. The appointment of a second trustee is unnecessary.

7.4.4 Beneficial tenants in common

Where co-owners are holding on trust for sale for themselves as beneficial tenants in common, the right of survivorship will operate as regards the legal title but *not* as regards the beneficial title. The deceased's beneficial share forms part of their estate and passes to their PRs.

A disposition by the sole surviving co-owner acting alone will be effective to transfer the legal title and their own share of the beneficial title but the buyer will still be subject to the beneficial interest of the deceased's estate.

To avoid this, the buyer should insist on the appointment by the survivor of a *second trustee*. The buyer who pays the purchase money to two trustees will then take free from the interest of the deceased's estate. The beneficial interest is overreached and the PRs must claim the deceased's share of the proceeds of sale from the two trustees.

Type of beneficial holding 7.4.5

How does a buyer know whether joint proprietors are holding for themselves as beneficial joint tenants or as tenants in common, or whether they are holding on trust for other beneficiaries?

The right of a beneficiary under a trust for sale is a minor interest. The principal device for protecting a minor interest is a restriction, although a caution can also be used (*see* Chapter 2, para. 2.2.2). Where a co-ownership restriction appears in the Proprietorship Register a buyer should not deal with a sole survivor but should insist on the appointment of a second trustee.

Where there is no such restriction a buyer is entitled to assume that the co-owners held as beneficial joint tenants and that a sole survivor therefore has sole legal and beneficial title and consequently that the appointment of a second trustee is unnecessary.

When co-owners apply for registration of title, the Land Registry asks how the beneficial title is held and unless they hold for themselves as beneficial joint tenants a restriction will be entered. If a beneficial joint tenancy is later severed a restriction must be entered.

You must, however, always be alert to the possibility that someone else who is not on the legal title may have a beneficial interest. If there is a caution protecting such an interest or if there is anyone with such an interest in occupation, the appointment of a second trustee will be necessary.

Summary 7.4.6

1 If a *joint proprietor dies* a buyer never needs to deal with the deceased's PRs.

2 If the proprietors held only for themselves as beneficial joint tenants a buyer can deal with the sole surviving proprietor alone.

3 If the proprietors held for themselves as beneficial *tenants in common* a buyer should insist on the sole survivor appointing a second trustee.

4 If the proprietors held for *beneficiaries other than themselves* a buyer should insist on the sole survivor appointing a second trustee.

Note

If there is more than one surviving proprietor in situations 3 and 4, nothing further needs to be done as there are still two trustees. Also, if the surviving trustee is a trust corporation, the appointment of a second trustee is not necessary, but this is not a situation which is often encountered in normal residential conveyancing.

5 If the sole surviving proprietor dies then a buyer will have to deal with that proprietor's PRs. (*See* Chapter 18, para 18.1.)

7.4.7 Beneficial interests which are not overreached

Where a buyer does not pay the purchase money to a minimum of two trustees or a trust corporation and thereby overreach any beneficial interests, it does not automatically follow that the buyer will be bound by a beneficial interest. For such an interest to bind the buyer it must either:

- Be *protected as a minor interest* by some entry on the Register; or
- Constitute an *overriding interest.*

As a *minor interest* it could be protected by the entry of a restriction or a caution. In either case the purpose of the entry is to alert the buyer to the existence of the interest and the need to overreach it. If, however, the overreaching machinery is not utilised the buyer will take subject to the protected interest.

If the interest is not protected as a minor interest it may nevertheless be protected as an *overriding interest* under s.70(1)(g), LRA 1925.

Note

This will only apply if the beneficiary is in occupation at the time of the transfer: *Abbey National Building Society v Cann* (1991).

If the buyer is bound by a beneficial interest it will mean that the beneficiary is not only entitled to a share in the value of the property but is also entitled to occupy it.

7.5 Dispositions by mortgagees

The proprietor of a registered charge has a power of sale: s.101, LPA 1925.

7.5.1 When does the power arise?

The power arises when the debt is due. You must therefore

examine the mortgage deed to see when this occurs.

Building society mortgages generally provide for the debt to be regarded as due, and therefore for the power of sale to arise, on a specific date shortly after the mortgage is created. *Bank* mortgages will provide for the debt to be payable on demand.

Provided that the power of sale has arisen, a buyer need not be concerned as to whether or not it has become exercisable under s.103 or any modification thereof contained in the mortgage deed: s.104, LPA 1925.

Note

If you are acting for a mortgagee who is selling, you must be sure that the power has become exercisable. If you do not, your client will be liable to the mortgagor for the premature exercise of the power.

Order for possession 7.5.2

In order to sell the property with vacant possession a mortgagee will (unless the mortgagor voluntarily vacates) first have to obtain a court order for possession. Under s.36, Administration of Justice Act 1970, the court has discretion to adjourn the proceedings for such period as it thinks reasonable where it considers that the mortgagor is likely to be able to pay the accrued sum, or remedy the breach of any other obligation under the mortgage, within a reasonable period.

Effect of a sale by mortgagee 7.5.3

A legal mortgagee is able to transfer the mortgagor's legal title: s.88(1), LPA 1925. As the buyer obtains title through the mortgagee the buyer will only be subject to third party interests that bound the mortgagee. If subsequent to the creation of the mortgage other incumbrances have been created, they will not bind the mortgagee, or the buyer from the mortgagee, even if they have been entered in the Register. In particular, the buyer will take free from any *later mortgages*.

Sale by a mortgagee realises the security but the mortgagor remains liable for any part of the debt which is still outstanding. As the security has been realised the charge over the property has been extinguished and it is unnecessary for the buyer to lodge a Land Registry Form 53 to obtain its removal from the Register.

Second mortgages 7.5.4

A sale by a first mortgagee extinguishes the second mortgagee's security, although the second mortgagee is of course still entitled to repayment of the outstanding debt. If the proceeds of sale are more than sufficient to repay the first mortgagee, the second mortgagee is entitled to the balance. Anything left after the second mortgagee has been repaid must be paid to the mortgagor (or subsequent mortgagees if there are any).

A sale by a second mortgagee will be subject to the first mortgage. To avoid this the second mortgagee will either pay off the first mortgagee or, where sufficient monies will be realised, persuade the first mortgagee to sell. The property can then be sold free of both mortgages.

7.5.5 Equitable mortgages

An equitable mortgage of a registered title can be created by the registered proprietor lodging their land certificate with a creditor with an accompanying memorandum which satisfies s.2, Law of Property (Miscellaneous Provisions) Act 1989 (*see* Chapter 10, para. 10.2). It will be protected by the entry of a notice of deposit in the Charges Register.

Such an arrangement is generally entered into to cover an informal short-term borrowing and it will avoid incurring Land Registry fees for registering a registered charge. (It is not commonly encountered in day-to-day residential conveyancing.) Such a mortgagee can only sell by first obtaining a court order for sale or converting the equitable mortgage into a registered charge. For example, a borrower may execute a registered charge at the outset but the lender may initially not register it but merely retain the land certificate and lodge a notice of deposit. Should it subsequently become necessary to realise the security, the charge can then be registered.

7.6 Third party rights

This section will consider the action you, as buyer's solicitor, must take when certain third party rights are encountered.

7.6.1 Mortgages

These can be removed by the seller paying them off. When this is done the mortgagee issues a Land Registry Form 53 which acknowledges the payment and the discharge of the security. It is lodged at the Land Registry to obtain the removal of the charge from the Register.

Note

You must obtain from the seller's solicitor a Form 53 for *each* outstanding mortgage.

Beneficial interests 7.6.2

If someone who is not on the legal title has a beneficial entitlement, you must ensure that the purchase money is paid to at least two trustees (or to a trust corporation). The beneficial interest will then be overreached and the buyer will take free from it.

An alternative is to get the beneficiary to join in the contract to agree to the sale and to waive their beneficial interest.

MHA rights 7.6.3

A spouse's right of occupation under the MHA must be protected by a notice on the Register; it can *never* obtain protection as an overriding interest. If protected by notice, it cannot be overreached.

Note

1 A spouse who is on the legal title does not have a MHA right. They don't need it.

2 The MHA gives a right to occupy but does not give a right to a share in the value of the property.

3 A spouse who has contributed to the value of the property will, in addition to the MHA right, have a beneficial interest which must be separately dealt with by overreaching it.

For the buyer to take free from the MHA right you must ensure that it is removed from the Register. This will require an application to the Land Registry for its removal signed by the spouse who entered it. If the notice exists pre-contract, you should not exchange contracts unless you are certain that the seller can secure its removal, ie. that the seller already holds the removal form signed by the spouse. The notice might, however, be entered after contracts have been exchanged. In this case, you must not complete until the MHA notice is removed or you receive an application form for its removal signed by the spouse who entered it.

Section 4, MHA 1983, provides that where there is a sale with vacant possession it is an implied term of the contract that the seller will secure the cancellation of any MHA charge. A seller will often have to give a spouse some financial inducement to remove it.

If the seller cannot secure the removal of the entry, the seller will be in breach of contract and the buyer will be entitled to refuse to complete.

Example

In *Wroth v Tyler* (1974) a husband with sole legal title contracted to sell the property. His wife registered an MHA charge and refused to remove it. The buyer sued the seller for damages for breach in failing to give vacant possession and was awarded very substantial damages, being the difference between the sale price and the greatly increased value of the property at the time of judgment.

A large award of damages could bankrupt a seller. Although the bankruptcy would not immediately extinguish the MHA right, the trustee in bankruptcy would be entitled to apply to the court for an order of sale and after 12 months the court must consider the creditors' interests as paramount: s.336, Insolvency Act 1986. The spouse's MHA right would then be lost anyway

Whenever the property is in just one spouse's name, it is advisable to get the other spouse to join in the contract to agree to give vacant possession. If they then fail to remove the notice (or register a notice), they will themselves be in breach of contract. If they also have a beneficial interest in the property, the contract can also provide for them to waive that interest.

7.6.4 Covenants and easements

Covenants and easements are burdens on the property which should be disclosed by the seller and the sale made subject to them. Generally nothing can be done to remove them and the buyer must therefore decide whether or not to buy such a property. Occasionally the person with the benefit of these rights will be prepared to relinquish them and enter into a deed of discharge.

In certain circumstances, eg. where restrictive covenants are obsolete, application may be made to the Lands Tribunal under s.84, LPA 1925, for their discharge or modification but this is a lengthy process and is therefore not viable if you are hoping to complete the purchase within a reasonable time.

Sometimes the Charges Register contains a notice of covenants affecting the property but does not give any details. This is because on first registration the title deeds revealed the existence, but not the details, of some covenants. In such a situation the seller must disclose that they are selling subject to these unknown covenants and the buyer will have to take it or leave it.

Where details of covenants are unknown, or where there is an outstanding breach of covenant, it is possible to insure against the risk of someone with the benefit of the covenant seeking to enforce it. Certain companies specialise in providing this restrictive covenant insurance and similarly in providing defective title insurance when there is some defect in the seller's title.

Cover is purchased by the payment of a one-off premium and it will be a matter for negotiation as to whether seller or buyer pays for it, but once acquired the benefit of the insurance can be passed on to later buyers.

Estate contracts 7.6.5

Sometimes an estate contract entry in the Register is, on investigation, found to be protecting a contract which no longer exists as the contract has been discharged. The seller should then secure its removal. If the entry is a 'live' entry the buyer will be bound by it.

Local land charges 7.6.6

The buyer will be subject to them. Although financial charges can be removed by the seller paying them off, other types cannot generally be removed.

Self-assessment questions

1 A seller of a registered title must deduce title in accordance with s.110, Land Registration Act 1925. What does this require of the seller?

2 What is the buyer's solicitor looking for when they investigate title?

3 When should a buyer's solicitor insist on the seller appointing a second trustee?

4 A mortgagee does not own the freehold title so how can they sell it to a buyer and why will the buyer take free from certain incumbrances which would have bound them had they bought from the mortgagor?

Chapter 8

Drafting the contract

Who does what? 8.1

The seller's solicitor drafts the contract of sale and sends two copies to the buyer's solicitor, keeping a further copy on file for reference purposes. Amendments may be negotiated over the telephone or by correspondence. If on the telephone, it is important that both sides keep an accurate attendance note of the conversation and that what was agreed is confirmed in writing. All agreed amendments are incorporated by the buyer's solicitor into the two copies of the contract which they hold. It is vital that the two copies are identical.

The buyer's solicitor returns one copy of the contract containing the agreed amendments to the seller's solicitor so that each side can sign one part of the contract. When both sides are ready to be legally bound the signed parts of the contract will be exchanged.

Note

The parties become legally bound not when they sign but at the moment of exchange.

The form and content of the contract 8.2

The contract has to be in writing, incorporate all the agreed terms and be signed by both parties: s.2, Law of Property (Miscellaneous Provisions) Act 1989. The parties can draft their own form of contract as no particular form is required but generally a set of standard terms is used with amendments and additions being made as the circumstances require.

The Standard Conditions of Sale 8.2.1

These conditions of sale have been approved by the Law Society and can be used for all types of sale, ie. for registered or unregistered titles, freehold or leasehold titles, domestic or commercial properties.

Note

Throughout this course you can assume that the contract incorporates the Standard Conditions of Sale. Special conditions are added to amend or supplement the Standard Conditions as appropriate.

8.2.2 The open contract

There are various statutory and common law implied terms which will operate in the absence of any contrary agreement. These are known as the open contract rules. For example, if a contract says nothing about whether a deposit is payable on exchange, then under the open contract rules no deposit is payable.

Note

A knowledge of the open contract rules is essential in order to appreciate what provisions need to be expressly stated in the contract. They will be referred to in context as appropriate in this companion.

8.3 Preparation for drafting the contract

In order to draft the contract, the seller's solicitor must first take certain preparatory steps.

8.3.1 Land/charge certificate

Obtain from the seller the land certificate or, if the property is mortgaged, the charge certificate from the mortgagee. If there is more than one mortgage on the property then all the charge certificates should be obtained as they will all have to be handed over to the buyer at completion.

To obtain a charge certificate, the seller's solicitor will need to give the mortgagee an undertaking to hold the certificate to the mortgagee's order and they must therefore return it at any time should the mortgagee require it.

8.3.2 Office copy entries

Complete Land Registry Form 109 to obtain from the relevant district land registry a full set of office copy entries, including a copy of the filed plan. The office copy entries will show the current state of the Register.

8.3.3 Overriding interests

Check for any overriding interests that incumber the property. This will be done primarily by questioning the seller, eg. asking who else is in occupation of the property, or has rights over it.

8.4 The seller's common law duty of disclosure

The open contract rule is that it is an *implied term* of the contract that the seller is selling an absolute freehold title free from incumbrances. If the title is not absolute and/or if there are any incumbrances/burdens on the property which will bind the buyer, these should be disclosed by the seller.

Extent of the common law duty 8.4.1

The duty of disclosure it limited to disclosing *latent* defects in/or burdens on the title, so there is in theory no duty to reveal patently obvious matters. However, there may well be room for argument as to whether or not a particular burden is patent or latent. Thus, to be on the safe side, the seller should disclose all defects and burdens.

Similarly, there is no duty to disclose matters that the buyer already knows about but, again there could be argument as to what the buyer did or did not know at the time of exchange of contracts. The fact that a particular incumbrance is registered, eg. as a local land charge, is not enough at the pre-contract stage to fix the buyer with knowledge of it, so the seller should disclose it.

At common law the seller's duty is absolute. It is a duty to disclose *all* latent defects and incumbrances that are not already known to the buyer and is not limited to matters that the seller knows or ought to know about.

Note

The duty of disclosure does *not* extend to anything relating to the physical state of the property. Here the rule is *caveat emptor* (let the buyer beware). However, if the buyer actually asks questions about the physical state of the property they must be answered truthfully otherwise the seller will be liable for misrepresentation.

Breach of the duty 8.4.2

Non-disclosure constitutes a breach of the implied term. It will depend on the seriousness of the breach whether the buyer's remedy is only damages, ie. for breach of warranty, or whether the buyer may also terminate the contract, ie. for breach of condition.

Modifying the common law duty 8.4.3

The Standard Conditions modify the common law duty of disclosure both as regards the extent of the duty and the consequences of non-disclosure (*see* Standard Conditions (SCs) 3.1 and 7.1).

The standard contract form 8.5

The Standard Conditions of Sale can be incorporated into your own form of contract or you can use a pre-printed contract form, the front page of which will have to be completed and special conditions added to the back of the form as appropriate. The following discussion assumes that you are using the standard form.

8.5.1 The agreement date

This will be left blank when the contract is initially drafted and only inserted when contacts are finally exchanged.

8.5.2 The parties

The full names and present addresses of sellers and buyers are inserted.

8.5.3 Property

The description of the property to be sold is sometimes referred to as the 'particulars of sale'. In the case of registered titles this part of the contract form can be completed by simply taking the description of the property from the property section of the Register and also stating the title number.

If the title is not an absolute one this must be clearly stated.

Delete the printed words 'leasehold' and 'root of title'.

8.5.4 Incumbrances on the property

This is where third party burdens that are going to bind the buyer should be disclosed. Look at the charges section of the Register to see what notices there are of third party rights and then state that the property is sold subject to those entries, eg. 'subject to entries numbers 1 and 2 on the Charges Register'. Where there are registered charges listed in the Charges Register, the seller will be discharging these, at or before completion, and they will not therefore bind the buyer. Consequently, they should not be stated as incumbrances subject to which the property is sold.

If there are overriding interests affecting the property these too constitute incumbrances and must be disclosed.

If there is insufficient room on the front of the agreement to set out all the incumbrances, the front page can simply state that the property is sold subject to the incumbrances set out in a special condition. Then on the reverse of the form, and on a separate sheet if necessary, the incumbrances can be set out in full.

Note

Apart from the incumbrances specifically mentioned on the face of the contract, the property is also sold subject to the incumbrances specified in Standard Condition 3.1.2 (*see* 8.7.3).

The pre-printed Special Condition 2 on the reverse of the form states that the property is sold subject to the incumbrances on the property and the buyer will raise no requisitions on them. This means that once contracts have been exchanged the buyer cannot raise questions about the incumbrances. The buyer must therefore ensure that all details of the incumbrances are supplied prior to the exchange of contracts and that any questions that the buyer wishes to raise are raised at the *pre-contact stage*. The seller will, of course, supply with the draft contract a set of office copy entries and where there are overriding interests affecting the property then the seller must provide such documentation as exists or oral information regarding them: s.110, Land Registration Act 1925.

Completion date 8.5.5

This will be left blank until just before exchange of contracts when the parties agree on the completion date.

The contract rate 8.5.6

If completion does not take place at the contractually agreed date, the party responsible for the delay will have to pay compensation to the other. This is calculated at the contract rate on the purchase price (*see* Standard Condition 7.3). The rate of interest can be stated by reference to a clearing bank's base rate, eg. 4% above the base rate from time to time of Lloyds Bank plc, or can be stated as being the Law Society contract rate. The Law Society rate is fixed at 4% above Barclays Bank's base rate and is published each week in the *Law Society Gazette*.

The purchase price 8.5.7

The full purchase price is inserted followed by any deposit that is to be payable on exchange of contracts. The customary deposit is 10%. If any chattels are being purchased for a separate consideration, ie. they are not included in the overall sale price, then the amount payable for chattels should be separately stated. The balance will be the balance of the purchase price less the deposit payable on exchange, plus any separate amount payable for chattels.

Title guarantee 8.6

The contract will state whether the seller will be transferring the property with full title guarantee, with limited title guarantee, with some variant of these or with no guarantee at all.

Depending on the type of guarantee given, certain covenants for title will be implied into the transfer by virtue of the Law of Property (Miscellaneous Provisions) Act 1994. These implied covenants are important to the buyer if a title problem arises after completion. It will then be too late to sue the seller for breach of contract and the buyer must therefore seek their remedy in the covenants impliedly given in the transfer (*see* Chapter 13, para. 13.4).

For over a hundred years prior to the 1994 Act sellers transferred in certain capacities, eg. as beneficial owners, trustees, personal representatives or mortgagees, and covenants for title were implied according to the capacity in which they transferred, the covenants being more extensive where someone transferred as beneficial owner than where they did so in the other capacities.

Note

In documents executed prior to 1 July 1995 (the date on which the 1994 Act came into operation) you will find no mention of full or limited title guarantee but will find sellers stating the capacity in which they acted.

8.6.1 The scope of the new covenants

Whether the seller gives a *full or limited title guarantee* they covenant that they:

- Have the right to dispose of the property as they purport to do;
- Will at their own cost do all that they reasonably can do to give the person to whom they dispose of the property the title they purport to give. This includes assisting with any queries that the Land Registry may raise in the buyer's application for registration: s.2.

If they give *full title guarantee* they also covenant that they:

- Are disposing of the property free from all charges and incumbrances (whether monetary or not) and from all other rights exercisable by third parties other than charges, incumbrances and rights which they do not and could not reasonably be expected to know about: s.3(1).

If they give *limited title guarantee* they also covenant that they:

- Have not since the last disposition for value created a charge or incumbrance which is still subsisting or granted third party rights over the property which are still subsisting or suffered the property to be so subjected and that they are not aware that anyone else has done so: s.3(3).

Which guarantee will be given? 8.6.2

Under the old system sellers transferred as beneficial owners, trustees, etc. without paying close regard to the implied covenants that they were thereby giving and whether or not they should be modified. This was probably because the covenants were so wordy that few people fully understood them! The new covenants are much shorter and easier to comprehend but a conscious decision now has to be taken as to the type of title guarantee which is to be given.

It would seem that beneficial owners should generally be able to give full title guarantee although they may be tempted to try to vary the guarantee by providing that the covenant set out in s.3(1) of the Act does not extend to any charge, incumbrance or other right which the transferor does not know about, ie. excluding any guarantee regarding matters that they might otherwise be reasonably expected to know about.

Note

Any modifications of the implied covenants must expressly refer to the section of the 1994 Act in which the covenant being modified is set out.

If the seller is a trustee, personal representative or mortgagee, they will probably only offer limited title guarantee. This may well alarm the buyer. The seller's solicitor should consider whether full title guarantee, limited in the way outlined in the previous paragraph, might be offered. Ultimately, a seller's ability to limit or exclude the implied covenants will depend on the relative bargaining strengths of the parties.

Note

If the contract makes no provision as to title guarantee, Standard Condition 4.5.2 provides that the seller is to transfer the property with full title guarantee.

The implied covenants for title are given not only by sellers to buyers but also by mortgagors to mortgagees and buyers' mortgagees will almost certainly insist that mortgagors give full title guarantee.

Note

The implied covenants are subject to the terms of the disposition and they will therefore not apply to defects and/or incumbrances to which the sale was made subject by the terms of the disposition (*see* s.6, 1994 Act).

8.7 Analysis of certain standard conditions of sale

8.7.1 Standard Condition 2.2: Deposit

Amount and purpose

The open contract rules do not provide for the payment of any deposit but Standard Condition 2.2 provides for a deposit of 10% to be paid no later than the date of the contract. If this figure is to be varied, a special condition needs to be added. Nowadays, deposits of 5% are very common.

The deposit acts as a partial payment so that, at completion, the buyer will only have to pay the balance of the purchase price. It also serves as a guarantee that the buyer will complete. If the buyer breaks the contract by failing to complete, then the seller will be able to retain the deposit. This is so even though the seller may suffer no loss as a result of the breach because the property can be resold at the same or a higher price.

Note

A seller's solicitor should not agree to the deposit being less than the normal 10% without the client's express authorisation as in the event of the buyer defaulting there will then be a smaller deposit to be forfeited. Where the seller suffers a loss as a result of the buyer's default, the reduced deposit may not cover that loss, whereas the normal 10% might have done so. The solicitor could be sued for negligence for the shortfall.

Agent or stakeholder

The deposit is not normally paid to the seller personally but to a third party, eg. the seller's solicitor. There are two capacities in which a third party may receive a deposit, either as agent for the seller or as a stakeholder.

If it is received as *agent for the seller* then the seller can ask for it to be handed over and may use it for any purpose, not necessarily for use in connection with a related purchase. There could then be problems for the buyer if the seller defaults and fails to complete. In such circumstances the buyer is entitled to the return of the deposit, but if the seller has already spent it, there may be problems in recovering the amount.

A *stakeholder* holds the deposit as agent for both parties to await the outcome of the transaction. If completion takes place, or if the buyer defaults, the stakeholder will pay the deposit to the seller. If the seller defaults, the stakeholder will return the deposit to the buyer.

From the buyer's point of view the stakeholder basis is

preferable, but the practical reality is that the seller may need to use the deposit money as a deposit on a related purchase and therefore needs to receive it on an agency basis. Under the open contract rule a solicitor receives a deposit as agent for the seller, but Standard Condition 2.2 modifies this and reaches a compromise solution under which the deposit can be used as a deposit on the purchase of another residence but not for any other purpose, and if not so used it is to be held on a stakeholder basis.

Possible problems

A practical problem may arise where contracts are exchanged under Law Society Formula B (*see* Chapter 10, para. 10.2). This incorporates an undertaking to forward the deposit by the following day but it is frequently not fulfilled as in a chain situation the buyer is relying on receiving the deposit on a related sale and then passing it on up the chain. There appears to be no satisfactory solution to this problem.

A further problem arises where the deposit is paid by a cheque which bounces. Standard Condition 2.2.4 makes it clear that the requirement that a deposit be paid is a term of the contract and not a condition precedent to the existence of the contract. It provides that the seller may either treat the contract as discharged by the breach or treat it as subsisting and sue for the deposit.

Standard Condition 9: Chattels 8.7.2

This makes it clear that, regardless of whether or not a separate price is paid for the chattels, there is in addition to the contract for the sale of land also a contract for the sale of goods. Under the sale of goods contract, ownership of the chattels will pass to the buyer on actual completion. The chattels being sold should be precisely listed and Special Condition 3 (on the reverse of the contract form) provides for this to be done in an attached list.

Conversely, if there are any fixtures which are not to be included in the sale, a special condition needs to provide for their removal.

The Protocol requires the seller to provide the buyer with a fixtures, fittings and contents form, and this will form part of the contract.

Standard Condition 3.1: Freedom from incumbrances 8.7.3

This states that the seller is selling the property free from incumbrances other than those mentioned in Condition 3.1.2. This specifies the incumbrances subject to which the property is sold, specifically:

- Those *mentioned in the agreement*, ie. those that have been expressly disclosed by the seller on the face of the contract;
- Those discoverable by *inspection of the property* before the contract, ie. those which are patently obvious.

  At common law the duty of disclosure is limited to the disclosure of latent incumbrances and this provision is therefore in line with the common law duty of disclosure. Many overriding interests will fall within this category;
- Those the seller *does not and could not know about.* At common law the seller's duty is to disclose all latent defects whether known about or not.

  This provision therefore constitutes a reduction of the common law duty but it is nevertheless regarded as an acceptable reduction.

Note

A provision that absolved the seller from the need to disclose matters that were actually known about would not be permissible.

- *Entries* made before the date of the contract in *any public register* except those maintained by HM Land Registry or its Land Charges Department or by Companies House.

  This seeks to fix the buyer with knowledge of matters registered in the local land charges register and public registers other than those specified. In *Rignall Developments v Halil* (1987) Millett J refused to equate *notice* imposed under s.198, Land Charges Act 1925 with the *knowledge* of the buyer which would preclude the seller's duty of disclosure. He held that notice and knowledge were not synonymous and that a seller with knowledge of a local land charge was under a duty to disclose it even though it was registered and therefore discoverable by a buyer. By expressly stating that the sale is subject to what is in these registers SC 3.1 seeks to put the onus of discovery on the buyer. Before exchanging contracts the buyer must search these registers (*see* Chapter 9, para. 5).
- *Public requirements* (defined in Standard Condition 1.1).

  The affect of this provision is uncertain. If the seller actually knows of the public requirement, it probably should be disclosed by specifying it in the agreement and the seller should not be able to shelter behind this contractual provision. SC 3.1.3 provides that after the contract is made the seller is to give the buyer details without delay of any new public requirement. It would therefore be strange if SC 3.1.2(e) were interpreted to mean that the property was sold subject to public requirements that were known to the seller before contract but which were not disclosed.

Standard Condition 4: Proof of title 8.7.4

Standard Condition 4.2.1 modifies s.110, Land Registration Act 1925 (*see* Chapter 7, para. 7.1.1) and requires the seller to provide office copies.

Standard Condition 4.1.1 provides for the proof of title to be delivered after exchange of contracts although this is increasingly unusual (*see* Chapter 7, para. 7.1.2).

Special conditions 8.8

These may be required to modify or supplement the Standard Conditions, eg. to specify fixtures to be removed or to modify the provisions regarding the deposit.

On a sale of the entirety of the land comprised in a registered title there is often no need for any special conditions, whereas on a sale of part there will usually be easements to be granted and reserved and covenants to be imposed. These will all be set out in special conditions (*see* Chapter 19).

Where the seller is deducing title before exchange of contracts there should be a special condition stating that title has been deduced and that the buyer will raise no further requisitions on the title.

Void conditions 8.8.1

The following conditions will be void if inserted in the contract:

- A condition restricting the buyer's choice of solicitor: s.48, LPA 1925.
- A condition restricting the buyer's right to object to any stamping deficiencies: s.117, Stamp Act 1891.

Self-assessment questions

1 What is the difference between the open contract rules and the Standard Conditions of Sale?

2 Why does the seller's solicitor need to investigate the seller's title before drafting the contract?

3 What is the purpose of a deposit and should it be paid to an agent of the seller or to a stakeholder?

4 If there are incumbrances on the property which are not specified in the contract:

(a) Will the buyer be bound by them?

(b) If their existence is discovered before completion, will the buyer be obliged to complete?

(c) If their existence is not discovered until after completion, will the buyer have any remedy?

Chapter 9

Pre-contract searches and enquiries

Introduction 9.1

It is the seller's duty at common law to disclose all latent defects in and incumbrances on the title. The seller is not obliged to disclose patent defects or incumbrances nor to disclose anything regarding the physical state of the property.

Standard Condition 3.1 seeks to modify the common law duty of disclosure and to absolve the seller from the duty to disclose matters that the seller does not and could not know about, and also entries on the register of local land charges and some other public registers (*see* Chapter 8, para. 8.7.3).

Their purpose 9.2

The buyer's pre-contract searches and enquiries are designed to find out about the physical state of the property and those title matters that the seller is not obliged to disclose, and also about a whole range of other matters that may influence the buyer's decision whether or not to buy, eg. whether the property enjoys mains drainage; whether there have been any disputes with the neighbours; whether a new motorway is planned near the property.

As a result of the pre-contract searches and enquiries the buyer may decide not to proceed at all, or may seek to negotiate a reduction in the price, or may insist on the draft contract being amended to incorporate some special condition.

Note

The buyer's solicitor will be negligent if they fail to make all appropriate searches and enquiries. It is therefore important to obtain from the client a clear picture of the type of property and its location. Obviously, this will be easier if the property is in the area in which you practise as you will be familiar with the area and aware of any particular local problems. On occasions you may need to go to look at the property so that you can fully understand a problem that has arisen, eg. over a boundary or right of way.

Pre-contract enquiries 9.3

Where the Protocol is *not* being followed, the buyer will send to the seller a list of pre-contract enquiries. The buyer may ask whatever they like and although there is no obligation on the seller to reply, if they refuse to do so the buyer will probably not proceed. If the questions are answered then the answers must be truthful. An incorrect reply may constitute an actionable misrepresentation.

Where the Protocol is being followed, the seller anticipates the usual questions that a buyer will raise and supplies the answers to those stock questions without waiting to be asked them. The questions are set out and the answers provided on the *property information form*. The seller's solicitor will need to go through this form with the client in order to obtain the information required to answer the questions.

Under the Protocol, the buyer may raise further enquiries but they should be kept to a minimum.

The standard pre-contract enquiries deal with the following matters.

9.3.1 Boundaries

The Land Registry operates a general boundary rule, ie. the Register and the filed plan give only a general indication of the extent of the property and do not give precise boundaries or state responsibilities for maintaining boundaries.

Standard Condition 4.3 provides that the seller need not prove the exact boundaries of the property or who owns fences, ditches, hedges and walls. Nevertheless the buyer will want to have as much information as possible with respect to boundaries and who maintains them.

Note

The pre-registration deeds can sometimes be useful in providing more detailed information about boundaries.

9.3.2 Disputes

The buyer does not want to buy a dispute. This question therefore asks whether there have been any disputes with the neighbours, either about the property which is the subject of the sale or about neighbouring properties. In *Walker v Boyle* (1982), for example, it was incorrectly stated that there had been no disputes with the neighbours when in fact there was an ongoing dispute. The buyer discovered the true position before completion and was able to rescind the contract for misrepresentation.

9.3.3 Notices

This asks what notices, if any, relating to the property have been served. Local authority notices regarding planning issues are the most frequently encountered notices.

Guarantees 9.3.4

The buyer wants to know what guarantees go with the property, eg. guarantees for central heating, double glazing, against dry rot or wood worm and, most importantly, any NHBC guarantee (*see* Chapter 6, para. 6.2).

Services 9.3.5

Mains services that run across private property do so by virtue of statutory rights. If, therefore, the property is served by mains services that run over someone else's land, the buyer does not have to worry about whether easements exist in respect of those services. Where the services are not mains services, easements in respect of them must exist and the buyer will need to be satisfied about this.

Facilities 9.3.6

This asks for details of shared facilities such as driveways and the cost of, and arrangements for, maintaining them.

Adverse rights 9.3.7

This question asks the seller to give details of all overriding interests and other rights affecting the property. In answering it, the seller will be going beyond the common law duty of disclosure and giving details not just of latent but also of patent rights.

Occupiers 9.3.8

This question to some extent overlaps with the previous question as, if there is someone in occupation who has rights in the land, those rights will constitute an overriding interest. When dealing with a sole seller, the buyer will be especially concerned to discover if there is anyone in occupation who has a beneficial interest in the property and, if so, will ensure that a second trustee is appointed so that on sale the beneficial interest is overreached. Anyone in occupation, even where their interest will be overreached, should be joined in the contract of sale in order to agree to vacate the property at completion. If they have so contracted, then they will probably vacate and this will avoid possible unpleasantness in having to evict them.

Restrictions 9.3.9

This seeks to discover whether there are any outstanding breaches of restrictions affecting the property and also to discover who has the benefit of restrictive covenants affecting the property.

9.3.10 Planning

This question refers to developments within the last four years as, if more than four years has elapsed since an unauthorised development other than change of user has occurred, a local authority can no longer serve an enforcement notice (*see* Chapter 6, para. 6.3.7).

9.3.11 Mechanics of sale

These questions about the seller's related transaction should only be answered by the seller's solicitor after receiving their *client's authorisation* to reveal the position.

9.3.12 Outgoings

This question is asked so that the buyer has a good idea of likely future liabilities in relation to the property.

9.4 Liability for misrepresentation

All answers given by the seller on the property information form must be correct. An incorrect answer will constitute a false statement of fact and, if it induces the buyer to make the contract (it need not be the sole inducement), it will constitute an operative misrepresentation. If the buyer discovers the misrepresentation pre-completion, the buyer may seek rescission, ie. restoration to the pre-contract position. At common law, the buyer may also be able to claim damages in tort for deceit or for negligence.

The Misrepresentation Act 1967, s.2(2) provides that where rescission is sought, but the misrepresentation was not fraudulent, the court may award damages in lieu of rescission. Section 2(1) of the Act provides that where the misrepresentation is not innocent, the party misled may claim damages as if the misrepresentation were fraudulent. This fiction of fraud can result in damages being recoverable for losses which would be considered too remote if the action were in negligence.

Note

In an action under s.2(1) the burden of proof is on the *defendant* to show that the misrepresentation was innocent. This contrasts with an action in tort where the burden of establishing fraud or negligence is on the plaintiff.

Standard Condition 7.1 seeks to modify the remedies that would otherwise be available for misrepresentation. It provides that the contract can only be rescinded where the error or omission results from fraud or recklessness, or where the injured party 'would be obliged to his prejudice to transfer or accept property differing substantially (in quantity, quality or tenure) from what the error or omission had led him to expect'. Whether this is reasonable under s.3, Misrepresentation Act 1967 has not yet been tested, but it probably is (*see* Chapter 13, para. 13.3).

Local land charges search 9.5

Under the Local Land Charges Act 1975, each local authority (LA) keeps a register of local land charges. It is divided into 12 classes. The vast majority of registrable charges consist of rights which the LA has in the property. There are also some statutory bodies which may have rights, eg. the Civil Aviation Authority. The only class of charge which can be entered by an ordinary person is a *light obstruction notice*. This is lodged in order to prevent a neighbour acquiring an easement of light by prescription.

Examples of local land charges 9.5.1

Examples include:

- *Financial charges*. These may be for a specific amount or general. For example, where a property has had the benefit of a local authority improvement grant there will be a charge for that amount which may have to be repaid if the property ceases to be used for residential purposes. Properties fronting a private unmade road may be subject to a charge for the making up and adoption of the road as a public highway.
- *Planning charges*, ie. where planning permission is granted subject to conditions.
- *Preservation orders* on buildings or trees.

The official search 9.5.2

The register is open to public inspection and a personal search can be made but an official search is usually instituted. The result of the search is not conclusive and registered charges which it fails to reveal, and local land charges which have not yet been registered, will still be binding. However, the advantage of the official search is that a buyer relying on an inaccurate search result will be entitled to compensation: s.10, Local Land Charges Act 1975. An official search also protects you, the solicitor, from a possible negligence claim.

Note

The buyer need not have instituted the search. It is sufficient that the buyer or their agent has knowledge of the contents of the official search certificate.

9.5.3 Search validation insurance

The official search does not carry with it any priority period. If a new charge comes into existence the day after the search, it will bind the property and the buyer.

To overcome this problem, a local search validation insurance scheme has been established by the Law Society for residential properties where the purchase price does not exceed £500,000. For a small premium the buyer will be compensated if there is any diminution in the market value of the property between the date of the search and the date of exchange of contracts as a result of new adverse charges. It is a condition of the insurance that contracts are exchanged within six months of the date of the search. The insurance also applies to the replies to the enquiries of the LA which are made on form CON 29.

9.6 Enquiries of the local authority

At the same time as the application for the local land charges search is submitted, enquiries about the property are made of the local authority on Form CON 29. These enquiries deal mainly with the status of the roads and drains which serve the property and with various planning matters.

The enquiries will reveal very little about matters beyond the property. To discover what plans there are for the surrounding area, eg. whether a petrol filling station is about to be built next door, other investigations will have to be made, such as asking questions of neighbours, residents' associations and staff at the LA offices. It is *not* part of the solicitor's normal function to undertake such investigations.

Note

The client must be advised of the limitations of the searches and enquiries which a solicitor normally makes. If your client has reason to suspect that there may be some particular problem in the surrounding area, you would normally assist in trying to obtain further information.

9.7 Special searches and enquiries

The location of the property may necessitate special searches and enquiries.

Common registration search 9.7.1

Registers of common land and town and village greens are kept by county councils. If the property adjoins an open space which might possibly fall into these categories then a search should be made to ensure that no part of the property is registered as publicly owned land.

Coal mining enquiries 9.7.2

If the property is in a mining area, enquiries should be made of The Coal Authority to discover:

- If there are any old, existing or proposed shafts, or other mine workings, in the vicinity of the property;
- Whether there is a risk of subsidence; and
- Whether any claim for subsidence damage has already been paid.

The Law Society produces guidance notes and a directory showing the areas of the country in respect of which enquiries should be made and a standard form for making them.

The buyer's solicitor will have to assess whether the replies to the enquiries necessitate further investigation and, if so, should explain to the client that specialist mining surveyors and structural engineers will be able to advise further.

Other mining enquiries 9.7.3

Similar enquiries should be made if the property is in an area where other minerals are abstracted from the land, eg. tin in Cornwall, salt in Cheshire, lead in the Yorkshire Dales.

Other special enquiries 9.7.4

There are many other special enquiries which may be appropriate in particular cases, eg. enquiring about flood levels if the property is near a river or enquiring about proposed railway lines.

Inspection of the property 9.8

This is important not only to discover what fixtures there are on the property, but also to discover overriding interests. At common law, the seller is not obliged to disclose patent incumbrances and, similarly, under Standard Condition 3.1.2 the property is sold subject to incumbrances discoverable by inspection of the property before contract even if they are not specifically mentioned in the contract.

Note

It is generally not practicable for the buyer's solicitor to inspect the property personally. The buyer's own inspection is relied on. However, you should advise the buyer as to what to look for, eg. evidence of anyone other than the seller being in occupation, and evidence of rights of way over the property.

An inspection is not the same as a survey (*see* Chapter 6, para. 6.1).

Self-assessment questions

1 What enquiries of the seller is the buyer entitled to raise pre-contract?

2 A buyer will be bound by overriding interests. How does a buyer discover what overriding interests, if any, exist?

3 What is the difference between the local land charges search and the enquiries of the local authority?

4 How will you know if special searches and/or enquiries are necessary?

Chapter 10

Exchange of contracts

Preparation for exchange: buyer 10.1

Before exchanging contracts you must be certain that the:

- *Terms of the contract* are satisfactory;
- *Investigation of title* (if title is deduced pre-exchange) and the results of all the *pre-contract searches and enquiries* are satisfactory;
- *Finance* for the purchase has been organised;
- *Client understands* all three issues above, has *signed* their part of the contract and has given you *authority* to agree the completion date and to exchange contracts.

Approval of the draft contract 10.1.1

The draft contract must be considered to ensure that it accords with your client's instructions and that its terms are appropriate to protect the buyer's interest and do not place excessive obligations on the buyer. The following questions in particular must be addressed:

- Are the names and addresses of all *parties* correctly stated? Should anyone else be made a party to the contract, eg. another trustee?
- Is the *property* correctly described, both as regards its physical description, including any plan, and the estate in it which is being sold?
- Is the *title guarantee* offered acceptable?
- Is the *price* correctly stated? If chattels are being sold are they to be included in the price or is there to be a separate consideration? Is there a list of all chattels which are being sold and of all fixtures which are excluded from the sale?
- Are the terms regarding the *deposit*, the *rate of interest* and the *time for completion* acceptable?
- Are special conditions which bar *requisitions* after exchange acceptable? Special Condition 2 of the Standard Agreement bars requisitions on the incumbrances (as defined in SC 3.1.2) and if the title has been fully deduced before exchange a special condition will probably bar all requisitions on title. If so, you must be sure that the title has been fully deduced, that you have fully examined it and that all requisitions previously made have been satisfactorily dealt with.

- *Special conditions*, especially those which modify the Standard Conditions, should be very carefully considered as they will invariably be for the seller's benefit.

Where amendments to the draft contract are negotiated and agreed, you must incorporate them in *both* copies of the draft contract and return one copy of the approved contract to the seller's solicitor.

10.1.2 Satisfactory investigations

The evidence of title must be satisfactory. This means not only being satisfied that the seller has the right to transfer the legal title but also being satisfied as to third party rights that the property enjoys or that incumber it. Specifically:

- Does the property have all *rights* necessary for its use and enjoyment, eg. rights of way to give access to the property for persons, animals and vehicles? Can they be used at all hours? Are there easements for existing services such as gas, electricity, drains and sewers and possibly for services one might wish to have in future such as cable television? Are any of these rights shared? What arrangements are there for their maintenance? Will there be any liability to contribute to the cost of maintenance?
- Are the *covenants* and *easements* which burden the property a problem? Will they impede the use which the buyer intends to make of the property or possible future development? Will they involve the buyer in expense, eg. maintaining drains that run across the property or maintaining boundary walls and fences?

  Although positive covenants are generally only directly enforceable against the original covenantor, they will be indirectly enforceable against the buyer if there is an indemnity chain. Will the buyer be required to give an indemnity? Standard Condition 4.5.4 provides that if after completion the seller will remain bound by any obligation affecting the property, the buyer is to covenant in the transfer to indemnify the seller against liability for any future breach of the obligation and to perform it from then on. Where a transferee enters into an indemnity covenant it will be noted in the Proprietorship Register so as to remind them of the need to obtain an indemnity when they come to sell.

Note

This helpful note is not entered by the Land Registry on a first registration. Consequently a first proprietor needs to look back at the conveyance to them to check whether they gave an indemnity and therefore need to take one from their successor.

- Are other *incumbrances* on the property going to be removed and, if so, is their removal assured?

The results of all the other pre-contract searches and enquiries must be satisfactory, eg. does it matter to the buyer that the property does not have mains drainage, or that the neighbours are noisy, or that even a small extension will require specific planning permission and will not be covered by the General Development Order?

Finance 10.1.3

The *purchase* may be financed by:

- The *proceeds* of sale of an existing property;
- The client's own *savings*;
- *Borrowing*, which will invariably be secured by a charge on the property.

Before *exchanging contracts* to buy you must be sure that:

- A *binding contract* for the sale of the existing property already exists or will come into existence at the same time as the purchase contract and that the completion dates and times are compatible;
- Any *savings* will be readily available in time for completion – notice to withdraw funds from an account may be necessary and other assets, eg. shares, may have to be realised;
- A satisfactory *mortgage offer* for the necessary amount has been made and accepted by the buyer. Are any of the conditions attached to the offer a problem, eg. is there the required NHBC cover? Will the funds be available when required? Will any retention being made cause difficulties?

As well as ensuring that the necessary finance will be available for completion, you must also ensure that the *deposit* is available immediately (*see* Chapter 8, para. 8.7.1). This may come from:

- The *deposit* on a related sale which has been paid over on an agency basis and can therefore be utilised;
- The client's own *savings*;
- A *bridging loan*. This is a temporary loan, generally from a bank, to bridge the gap until mortgage funds and/or the proceeds of a related sale are available. It must then be repaid. A bridging loan is very expensive and you should try to avoid having to resort to one.

Note

To enable your client to obtain bridging finance, you will be required to give the bank an undertaking for its repayment.

10.1.4 Signing the contract: buyer or seller

Before your client signs their part of the contract, you should go though it with them to ensure that they understand its main terms. In particular, they must appreciate that once contracts have been exchanged they are fully bound and that if they fail to perform their contractual obligations they will be in breach of contract and liable to compensate the other side.

When acting for the *buyer* you must also go through the results of your investigation of title and the pre-contract searches and enquiries and draw to your client's attention any problems which have arisen. Ensure that your client understands all relevant issues and that all their queries and concerns have been answered.

Also ensure that the buyer understands the terms of any mortgage offer and the effect of a mortgage, and that they are satisfied with the results of the survey.

Note

It is advisable to put in writing your information and advice regarding problematical issues.

When you are certain that your client understands all the issues and wishes to proceed, get your client to sign their part of the contract. Witnessing of their signature is unnecessary.

Note

A solicitor does not have implied authority to sign a contract on a client's behalf but could be expressly authorised, preferably in writing, to do so.

The signed contract is then left with you with authority to agree the completion date, within the limits laid down by your client, and to exchange contracts. You must be certain that you have your client's authority to exchange. Although a solicitor has ostensible/apparent authority to exchange contracts, and therefore an exchange effected by you will bind your client, if you do not actually have authority you will be liable to your client. If you do have your client's authority to exchange, it is implied that you may do so by any method which the law recognises as constituting an exchange: *Domb v Isoz* (1980).

10.2 Methods of exchange

10.2.1 Statutory requirements

Section 2, Law of Property (Miscellaneous Provisions) Act 1989, requires contracts for the sale or other disposition of an interest in land to be:

- *In writing;*
- Incorporate all the expressly agreed *terms;* and
- Be *signed* by each party.

Section 2 specifically recognises the practice of exchanging contracts and provides that all the terms must be set out in each part but the parties may sign separate parts.

Methods of exchange 10.2.2

Exchange of contracts involves the physical transfer of each signed part to the other side. However, even before the physical transfer occurs, a solicitor may acknowledge that they are holding their client's signed part of the contract on behalf of the other side and this will constitute an exchange.

An exchange may be made in various ways:

- *In person.*

  The solicitors meet and exchange their respective parts.
- By *post* or delivery to a *document exchange.*

  The contract comes into existence when the second part is posted: *see* SC 2.1.1. This creates uncertainty as how do you know which is the second part?
- By *telephone, telex.*

  This involves agreeing with the other side to hold your client's signed part on their behalf and undertaking to forward it to the other side. The exchange takes place from the moment the agreement is made on the telephone: *see* SC 2.1.2. The whole process depends for its effectiveness on the fact that it is underpinned by solicitors' undertakings.

Note

The vast majority of exchanges are effected over the telephone. It is the only method which is practicable where there is a chain involved and all parties wish to exchange as simultaneously as possible.

The Law Society formulae 10.2.3

To facilitate exchange by telephone/telex, the Law Society has drawn up three formulae which specify the obligations of the respective solicitors when effecting such exchanges. They are used in different factual situations.

- *Formula A* is used where one solicitor (usually the seller's) already holds both signed parts.
- *Formula B* is used where each solicitor holds their own

client's signed part of the contract. This is the most widely used formula.

- *Formula C* is specifically designed for use in chain transactions and is considerably more complex than the other two.

By referring to one or other of these formulae the solicitors incorporate them into their agreement and thereby determine the effect of their agreement and the terms of the undertakings which they impliedly give. (Details of the formulae are contained in the Law Society's *Guide to the Professional Conduct of Solicitors*.)

10.2.4 Dating the contract

Immediately before agreeing the exchange, the completion date must be agreed and inserted in each part of the contract and, following exchange, the date of exchange must be inserted in each part.

10.3 Conditional contracts

Although it is undesirable, contracts may sometimes be exchanged subject to a condition, eg. subject to a satisfactory local search or subject to obtaining planning permission.

The terms of the condition must be specific otherwise the whole contract will be void for uncertainty, eg. 'subject to survey' or 'subject to mortgage' would be too vague. 'Subject to planning permission' may also be too vague unless it can be construed as impliedly referring to a planning application which is pending. Where a condition is imposed a time limit for its fulfilment may be specified but if not it must be fulfilled by the completion date.

If the condition is not fulfilled the contract comes to an end; both parties are released from it and the buyer is entitled to recover the deposit. However, where the condition has been imposed for the benefit of one party only, that party may choose to waive its non-fulfilment and keep the contract in existence, eg. the buyer may waive the fact that the hoped-for planning permission has not been granted.

Self-assessment questions

1 What amendments to the draft contract is the buyer's solicitor entitled to make?

2 What should the buyer's solicitor do about any irremovable incumbrances which are discovered pre-exchange?

3 What is the purpose of a deposit; how much will it be;

where will the money come from and to whom should it be paid?

4 When does an exchange of contracts

(a) by post

(b) by telephone

take effect?

Chapter 11

Exchange to completion

The effect of a binding contract 11.1

From the moment that contracts are exchanged the parties are legally bound. A failure by either party to perform their obligations under the contract will constitute a breach entitling the other party to the usual contractual remedies (*see* Chapter 13). However, as with any other type of contract the parties may, by subsequent agreement, modify or terminate the contract.

Note

Any such subsequent agreement must comply with s.2, Law of Property (Miscellaneous Provisions) Act 1989 to be enforceable.

Protecting the buyer's equitable title 11.1.1

A binding contract for the sale of land does more than just create contractual rights and obligations. 'Equity regards that as done which ought to be done' and therefore from the moment of exchange the buyer has the equitable title. This equitable right of the buyer to have the legal estate transferred to them is known as an *estate contract*.

For this equitable right to bind a later purchaser of the legal estate, it must be protected as a minor interest by entering a notice or caution on the Register. However, unless the buyer has reason to suspect that the seller may subsequently enter into a contract with someone else, it is not usual to protect the buyer's estate contract where completion is planned to take place within a normal period of time, eg. within four weeks. Where there will be a longer period between exchange and completion, the estate contract should be protected immediately; it is also advisable to register the contract if completion is delayed.

Note

Any contract which includes an option or a right of pre-emption should always be protected straightaway.

The risk in the property 11.1.2

At common law the risk passes with the equitable title. If the property increases or diminishes in value between exchange and completion, that change is for the buyer's account. The property is also at the buyer's risk so far as physical damage is concerned so that the buyer must still perform the contract at the full price even though the property has been damaged. Even if the buildings standing on the land have been totally destroyed, the buyer cannot plead that the contract has been frustrated by the destruction of the subject matter as the land is still there, and that is the real subject matter of the contract.

As the buyer has the risk in the property, the buyer needs to have insurance cover from the moment of exchange. The seller also needs to maintain insurance cover on the property following exchange because if for some reason completion never takes place the seller will retain the property. Consequently, the property is often insured by both parties.

Unless the buyer is allowed into possession before completion, the seller is liable, as a qualified trustee, to take reasonable care to keep the property in its contract condition. The buyer may therefore have redress if damage to the property is the result of the seller's breach of duty, eg. if the seller vacates the property without making it secure.

11.1.3 Standard Condition 5.1

This seeks to remove the need for the buyer to take out insurance from exchange of contracts and so to avoid double insurance. Standard Condition 5.1 states that the seller retains the risk until *completion*.

Note

This refers only to the physical risk and the risk of a change in the value of the property is still with the buyer.

Standard Condition 5.1.1 provides that the seller will transfer the property in the same physical state as it was in at the date of the contract (except for fair wear and tear), ie. it imposes an *absolute* contractual obligation on the seller which is clearly far more beneficial to the buyer than the seller's common law duty as trustee to take reasonable care.

If the property is damaged the buyer will still have to complete, unless 5.1.2 applies, but will be able to claim damages from the seller for breach of Condition 5.1.1. Unfortunately, 5.1.3 provides that the seller is under no obligation to the buyer to insure the property.

The Protocol makes it clear that the buyer's solicitor must ensure that buildings insurance arrangements are in place. They should therefore ensure that a special condition is included which requires the seller to have adequate insurance in place until completion and which enables the buyer's interest to be noted on the policy. Alternatively, separate insurance may be taken out for the buyer, in which case SC 5.1 may be deleted entirely and the common law position restored.

Standard Condition 5.1.2 provides that if at any time before completion the physical state of the property makes it unusable for its purpose at the date of the contract, then the *buyer* may rescind the contract. The *seller* may rescind where the property has become unusable for that purpose as a result of damage against which the seller could not reasonably have insured or which it is not legally possible for the seller to make good. This is a sort of *force majeure* clause. If the property is so badly damaged that it cannot be used then the parties are released from the contract. The buyer will be entitled to the return of their deposit but the seller will not be liable for any damages.

Standard Condition 5.1.4 provides that s.47, Law of Property Act 1925 does not apply. Section 47 provides that in certain circumstances insurance money received by the seller is received on behalf of the buyer. It is not a very satisfactory section so far as protecting the buyer is concerned and most contracts of sale exclude it.

Occupation by the buyer 11.1.4

Although the seller holds the legal title on trust for the buyer, the seller is entitled to retain possession of the property until completion. They will be entitled to any income from the property and must bear all outgoings on it. Sometimes, however, the buyer is allowed into occupation before completion.

It is important to distinguish between allowing a buyer into *occupation* and allowing the buyer *access* to the property. Buyers are often allowed to go in and out of the property to measure up for curtains, carpets etc., or to get estimates for work to be carried out, and even for work to be done, but this does not normally amount to the buyer entering into occupation. While each case will depend on the particular circumstances, a vital factor would seem to be whether or not the buyer is allowed to *retain the keys*. If the keys have to be returned to the seller or the seller's agent after the work has been done, the buyer only has *access*, they have not been allowed into occupation.

The effect of the buyer entering into occupation is dealt with fully in Standard Condition 5.2. At common law the status of the buyer in occupation is not clear-cut and it might be difficult for the seller to remove the buyer if the buyer fails to complete. Also at common law, a buyer who enters into possession is presumed to be accepting the seller's title. Standard Condition 5.2.7 clearly negates this and preserves the buyer's right to question the seller's title and raise requisitions on it. SC 5.2.2 also makes it clear that the buyer is in occupation as a licensee and not as a tenant and has an obligation to insure the property.

11.2 Requisitions on title

Traditionally the seller deduces title and the buyer raises requisitions after exchange of contracts. Standard Condition 4.1 preserves this traditional approach and lays down a timetable for the raising and answering of requisitions.

If the seller refuses to answer a proper requisition the buyer can either rescind the contract or take out a vendor and purchase summons under s.49, LPA 1925 to compel an answer.

If the Protocol is adopted, title is deduced before exchange and it is usual in the case of registered titles for title to be deduced pre-contract even in cases where the Protocol is not being followed. Where title is deduced pre-contract the seller should ensure that the contract contains a special condition stating that this is being done and that the buyer is barred from raising requisitions once contracts have been exchanged.

In addition to true requisitions on title, there are also certain standard form requisitions which the buyer will always raise pre-completion. These standard form requisitions primarily deal with the arrangements for completion. In particular, they ask for details of the client account of the seller's solicitor, to which payment of the price is to be made, and whether any existing mortgage will be discharged prior to completion and a Form 53 provided, or whether an undertaking will be offered instead. If the buyer's solicitor wishes the seller's solicitor to act as agent on completion (*see* Chapter 12, para. 12.4.1), this is also requested.

11.3 Preparing documentation

In preparation for completion there are various documents that need to be drafted.

11.3.1 The Land Registry transfer

Legal estates must be transferred by deed and for registered titles there are prescribed Land Registry Forms. In the case of a transfer of the entirety of the land Form 19, or Form

19(JP) if there are joint purchasers, will be used.

The *transfer* contains:

- The *title number* and *description* of the property.
- The *date* of the transfer.
- *Consideration and receipt clause.* The Stamp Act 1891 requires the consideration to be accurately stated and it is on the basis of this figure that any stamp duty liability will be calculated. It is only the consideration for the land which is stated. Where there is a separate consideration for chattels this is not mentioned.

Note

The receipt element of the clause is important in two respects.

First, the fact that the transfer is drafted incorporating a receipt clause serves as authorisation to the buyer to pay the purchase price to the seller's solicitor, ie. the presence of the receipt clause holds out the seller's solicitor as authorised to receive the purchase money.

Second, the receipt clause serves as a sufficient receipt to the buyer who does not therefore need to obtain a separate receipt. This is particularly important where the money is being received by trustees as the receipt by them of the purchase price activates the overreaching machinery.

- *Seller's name and address.*
- The operative words 'hereby transfers' and a statement indicating whether *full title* or *limited title* guarantee is being given (*see* Chapter 8, para. 8.6).
- *Buyer's name and address.*
- The *description of the property transferred* as being all the property registered under the specified title number.
- An express *indemnity covenant*. This is included where the sale is subject to existing restrictive covenants and the contract requires the buyer to give the seller an indemnity in respect of the seller's continuing liability on those covenants.

  The seller will remain liable on the covenants if they are either the original covenantor or if they have themselves given an indemnity in respect of the covenants to their predecessor. Standard Condition 4.5.4 provides that the buyer will not only covenant to indemnify the seller against liability for future breaches but will also covenant to perform the covenants. As a result the seller will be able to take direct action against the buyer to prevent a breach of covenant and not merely claim an indemnity if they themselves are held liable for the breach.

- *Co-owners* – where there is more than one purchaser there will be a statement as to whether the survivor can give a *valid receipt* or not. If the survivor can give a valid receipt it indicates that they are to hold as beneficial joint tenants, if not, as tenants in common. However, a statement that the survivor can give a valid receipt may not be conclusive that they are to be beneficial joint tenants and an express declaration should also be entitled.

Note

The transfer does not define the extent of the beneficial interests of tenants in common. These should be specified in a separate declaration of trust.

- *Certificate of value*, if appropriate (*see* Chapter 4, para. 4.2).
- *Execution and attestation* – both parties must sign the transfer and their signatures must be witnessed.

Execution takes place by signing the document as a deed and by delivering it. Delivery means an act done so as to indicate an intention to be bound. Handing the document over to the other side clearly does this but there can be a delivery without physical transfer of the document.

At one time, authority for an agent to deliver a deed had itself to be given by deed. This was rarely done. Consequently, when a seller signed a transfer and handed it to their own solicitor in readiness for completion, it was regarded as already having been delivered, although the delivery was conditional on the buyer paying the purchase price. A conditional delivery is known as a *delivery in escrow*. Once a conditional delivery has taken place, it must await the performance of the condition and the seller cannot withdraw the document.

Section 1, Law of Property (Miscellaneous Provisions) Act 1989 provides that authority to deliver a document as a deed need no longer be given by deed. It is therefore now possible for the deed to be left with the seller's solicitor with authority to deliver it on the client's behalf without this immediately constituting a conditional delivery.

Note

The seller can now have second thoughts and instruct their solicitor not to hand it over to the buyer.

Traditionally, the transfer document is drafted by the buyer's solicitor, sent to the seller's solicitor for approval and, when approved, engrossed, ie. retyped, by the buyer's solicitor. This process may be followed in the case of a deed of conveyance for an unregistered title but a Land Registry transfer, especially when it is one of the entirety of the title, is so straightforward that it is generally unnecessary to prepare a draft. The form is prepared by the buyer's solicitor, the buyer executes it and it is sent to the seller's solicitor for the seller to execute in readiness for completion.

The buyer's mortgage 11.3.2

If the mortgage is to an institutional mortgagee there will be no need to draft a mortgage deed as the institution's standard form will be used. The solicitor acting for the mortgagee must ensure that before completion the mortgage deed has been completed and executed by the buyer.

In good time before completion, the mortgagee's solicitor must send the mortgagee a Report on Title confirming that the title has been investigated and is good to lend against. If there are any problems with the title, these must be drawn to the mortgagee's attention.

At the same time as the mortgagee is sent the Report on Title, the solicitor requisitions, ie. requests, the mortgage money. Many mortgagees now send the money directly to their solicitor's client account by telegraphic transfer (TT) but some still send the money by cheque. The buyer's solicitor will need to clear the cheque through their client account before the funds can be utilised and therefore the cheque needs to be obtained a few days before completion to allow time for clearance. Some mortgagees will, as a matter of course, send the cheque a few days before completion but others will time it to arrive on the morning of completion unless asked for it earlier.

Note

The mortgagee will start charging interest on the mortgage advance from the date of the cheque. This means that the buyer will have to start paying interest on the mortgage money before completion has actually taken place. The reasons for this need to be carefully explained to the client well in advance.

If the mortgage is an *endowment* mortgage, the buyer's solicitor must ensure that before completion the life insurance policy has been taken out and that it is for the correct amount. If the mortgagee requires the benefit of the policy to be formally assigned, the solicitor must ensure that the buyer/mortgagor signs the necessary deed to assign the life policy to the mortgagee.

For an assignment of a life policy to take effect as a legal assignment the insurance company must be notified in writing of the assignment. The solicitor will therefore prepare two copies of a notice of assignment ready to send to the insurer's head office post-completion. One copy will be returned by the insurance company as its acknowledgement that the notice has been received.

11.3.3 The seller's mortgage: undertaking for Form 53

Where the seller has a mortgage on the property it will have to be discharged in order for the buyer to take free from it. The buyer is entitled to insist that this be done before completion so that on completion the seller's solicitor hands over Form 53 executed by the mortgagee.

This form is a receipt for the mortgage money and is lodged at the Land Registry to secure the removal from the Register of the registered charge. In practice the seller usually needs the sale proceeds to redeem the mortgage and if the buyer insists on the seller redeeming the mortgage before completion the seller may have to raise bridging finance to do so. This will be expensive for the seller. Consequently, the seller generally asks if the buyer will be prepared to complete on the basis of a solicitor's undertaking.

In the undertaking the solicitor must only promise to do things which are within their control, ie. to send off to the mortgagee the money to redeem the mortgage and to send to the buyer the Form 53, if and when it is received from the mortgagee. The solicitor cannot guarantee that the mortgagee will actually issue the Form 53. However, where the mortgagee is an institutional mortgagee, it is most unlikely that on repayment of the outstanding balance it will not issue the necessary Form 53. Buyers' solicitors are therefore generally prepared to complete on the basis of a solicitor's undertaking in the Law Society's approved form where the mortgage is to an institutional mortgagee.

In the case of a private mortgage, there is a risk that the mortgagee may fail to issue the Form 53 and therefore a buyer's solicitor should *not* agree to complete on the basis of an undertaking.

Where there is more than one mortgage on the property, the buyer's solicitor must ensure that all the mortgages will be discharged before completion or that a satisfactory undertaking, which covers all the mortgages, will be given.

The seller's solicitor must ensure that their undertaking refers to the specific mortgage(s) which they will redeem and does not unintentionally render them liable on others about which they are unaware.

Statements of account 11.3.4

Both solicitors should, before completion, send to their respective clients statements of account. In the case of the *seller* it will show what, if anything, will be left out of the proceeds of sale when all outstanding mortgages and the costs of the sale have been paid. In the case of the *buyer* it will show the purchase price plus all the costs of the purchase and will then set out how that is to be funded, eg. the proceeds of a related sale, the mortgage money, plus any balance to be provided by the buyer. Where the buyer has to provide funds to enable completion to take place then, if these are being provided by cheque, time must be allowed for the cheque to clear. The buyer's solicitor must therefore make it clear to the client that the cheque is required several days before the contractual completion date.

The statement to the buyer is sometimes preceded by a completion statement, issued by the seller's solicitor to the buyer's solicitor, setting out the amount required to complete the transaction. In a simple freehold transaction this is frequently dispensed with as what is required is simply the balance of the purchase price, ie. the price less the deposit already paid on exchange.

Note

The seller's failure to supply a completion statement does not justify the buyer's failure to complete. The buyer must still complete on the basis of offering what is believed to be the correct amount: *Carne v Debono* (1988).

Pre-completion searches 11.4

In preparation for completion the buyer's solicitor will need to make certain searches.

Search of the Land Register 11.4.1

A search will be made at the relevant district land registry on Form 94A. This is done to discover whether any new entries have been made since the date of issue of the office copies, which must not be more than 12 months earlier. A fee of £5 is payable.

The buyer will expect the search certificate to come back saying that there have been no adverse entries. If there are new adverse entries this may justify the buyer in refusing to complete or, at the very least, is likely to delay completion while the entries are investigated. The official search certificate is not conclusive in the buyer's favour and if there are entries which it fails to reveal the buyer will still be subject to them, but will be entitled to an indemnity from the Land Registry under s.83, LRA 1925.

The great advantage of the official search is that it gives a priority period of 30 *working* days. This means that provided the buyer completes and registers the transaction within that period they will not be affected by any further entries made after the date of the search.

11.4.2 Inspection of the property

There should, ideally, be a last minute inspection of the property, eg. by the client, to check that there is no one in occupation who might have an interest that would be protected under s.70(1)(g), LRA 1925, and that no fixtures have been removed.

11.4.3 Search of the local land charges register?

It is not usual to repeat this search unless there has been a particularly long period between exchange and completion, eg. something in excess of six months. Even then the purpose of the search is simply for the buyer's information and if there are new charges it will not justify the buyer in refusing to complete. The risk of new local land charges is on the buyer from the moment of exchange.

11.4.4 Search of the company's register?

Where the seller is a company, a search of the company's register is advisable. All charges, including floating charges, created by a company must be protected by entry on the Register of Title, otherwise the buyer will not be bound by them even if they are registered at Companies House. A company search will, however, reveal other information about the company such as whether it is in the process of being wound up.

11.4.5 Mortgagee's searches

The solicitor acting for the buyer's mortgagee must ensure that the searches already discussed are made. For the mortgagee to have the benefit of the priority period given by the Form 94A search, the search must be done specifically on behalf of the mortgagee. It will then allow 30 working days for the buyer to register the transfer and for the mortgagee to register the charge, and *both* will be protected against any new entries during this period.

The mortgagee's solicitor must also do a bankruptcy

search (Form K 16) against the name(s) of the prospective mortgagor(s), ie. the buyer(s). This is a search in the index to the registers which are maintained under the Land Charges Act 1972. It is not a full search of all the registers but is limited to bankruptcy entries, ie. bankruptcy petitions, bankruptcy orders and deeds of arrangement with creditors. If any such entry appears against a buyer's name, the mortgagee must immediately be notified and the mortgage advance will not be made. There will then almost inevitably be a failure to complete by the buyer who will be liable for breach of contract.

Self-assessment questions

1 If the property is damaged between exchange and completion what rights, if any, will the buyer have?

2 What is the difference between the contract of sale and the Land Registry transfer?

3 Why does not the buyer always insist on the seller paying off their outstanding mortgage before completion and how can the buyer then be sure that they will not be bound by the seller's mortgage?

4 What is the purpose and effect of the Form 94A Land Registry search and why, when the buyer is buying with the aid of mortgage, must the search by done in the mortgagee's name?

Chapter 12

Completion and post-completion

Completion defined 12.1

Completion is the performance of the contract. The buyer pays the price and the seller performs their side of the contract by putting the buyer in a position to acquire the legal title by applying for registration of the transfer.

Payment of the price 12.2

The buyer pays the price less any deposit already paid. If the deposit was paid over on an agency basis the seller will already have received it. If it was paid to a stakeholder, at completion the stakeholder can pay it to the seller without waiting to receive authorisation to do so from the buyer: *Hastingwood Property Ltd v Saunders Bearman Anselm* (1990).

By telegraphic transfer 12.2.1

The buyer's solicitor instructs their bank to make payment direct from their client account to the client account of the seller's solicitor. The standard requisitions on title will have obtained details of the bank and account number to be credited.

The transfer does not occur instantaneously and there can be a delay of several hours between the buyer's solicitor's bank being instructed to make the transfer and the seller's solicitor's bank receiving it. This can cause problems in a chain situation where the seller's solicitor is relying on the proceeds of sale to finance a related purchase.

The Solicitors' Accounts Rules prohibit the use, even for a short period, of funds in the client account belonging to other clients. You must therefore wait to receive the sale proceeds before you can pay out for your related purchase. To overcome this problem, you must make sure that the latest time for completion in your sale contract is considerably earlier than that in your purchase contract.

By banker's draft or in cash 12.2.2

A banker's draft is a promise of payment by a bank and it is regarded as being as good as cash. This method of payment involves the buyer's solicitor collecting from their bank a draft payable to the seller's solicitor's client account and delivering it by hand. It is only convenient to pay by this method if the completion is to be by personal attendance and even then it will rarely be used in a chain transaction.

Payment in cash is subject to the same constraints and is therefore rarely used.

12.2.3 Payment for chattels

Where chattels are purchased for a separate consideration, a separate receipt should be obtained from the seller, as the receipt embodied in the transfer is only for the price paid for the land.

12.3 Performance by the seller

Before paying over the price the buyer's solicitor must check that the seller is able to perform their side of the contract. This involves checking that:

- The seller's solicitor holds the *land certificate*, or *charge certificate* if there is an outstanding mortgage. There should be as many charge certificates as there are outstanding mortgages;
- A *Form 53* signed by the mortgagee will be handed over in respect of each outstanding mortgage or, if the buyer has agreed to complete on the basis of an undertaking from the seller's solicitor, that an *undertaking* in the Law Society's approved form is available;
- The Land Registry *transfer* is properly executed;
- Other *documents* which the seller has promised to supply are available, eg. NHBC documents, other guarantees that go with the property, planning consents; and
- A *receipt for chattels* purchased separately is available.

12.4 The completion process

What actually happens at completion?

- The *checks* listed in 12.3 are carried out;
- The *buyer pays* the price;
- The *transfer is dated* and *handed over* to the buyer's solicitor together with the other documents listed in 12.3;
- The *keys are handed over* or *authority given* to whoever holds them, eg. the estate agent, to release them;
- Where the buyer is purchasing with the aid of a mortgage, the *mortgage deed is dated* with the same date as the transfer and takes effect immediately.

Completion can take place either by *personal attendance* or by *post*. If by personal attendance someone, eg. a trainee solicitor, will be sent from the buyer's solicitor's office to the seller's solicitor's office to 'do the completion'. If the seller's solicitor is not nearby the buyer's solicitor may appoint another firm, in the same town as the seller's solicitor, as agent to do the completion. In both these situations, payment is likely to be made by banker's draft unless a chain transaction is involved

Note

In a chain transaction, completion by personal attendance is unusual even if the other solicitor is nearby.

A further possibility is that the seller's solicitor is appointed as agent to do the completion on the buyer's behalf as well as on the seller's behalf. This is known as completion by post and it is the most common method of completion. In this method, payment will always be made by telegraphic transfer.

Note

It seems that the general prohibition on acting for both seller and buyer does not apply to this arrangement but the possibility of a conflict of interest should always be considered. If it exists, this arrangement must be avoided, eg. if the buyer's solicitor suspects that the seller's solicitor may not be in a position to hand over the requisite documents.

The Law Society's Code for Completion by Post 12.4.1

The Law Society has drawn up a code of practice for postal completions which is set out in the *Solicitors' Guide to Professional Conduct*. The Code makes it clear that the buyer's solicitor must give precise instructions as to what the seller's solicitors is to do, eg. documents to be checked; documents to be forwarded. It specifies the obligations of the seller's solicitor and incorporates into the agency arrangement certain undertakings, eg. the seller's solicitor undertakes that they have authority from both the seller and the seller's mortgagee to receive the purchase money.

The Code itself states that it only applies if specifically adopted by the solicitors involved. However, if the Protocol is being followed, the Code will apply automatically unless otherwise agreed. Where the Protocol is not being followed, adoption of the Code is nevertheless usual and is provided for in the standard pre-completion requisitions.

12.4.2 The effect of completion

- As the title is already registered, legal title does not pass to the buyer on completion but only on registration of the transfer.
- The doctrine of merger operates (*see* Chapter 13) but probably not until the transfer is registered.

12.5 Post-completion

Each solicitor should immediately inform their client that completion has taken place and then deal with other post-completion matters.

12.5.1 Seller's solicitor

The seller's solicitor must:

- If acting as the buyer's agent on completion, comply with the obligation embodied in that arrangement and *forward documents* to the buyer's solicitor.
- If an undertaking has been given for the *discharge of an outstanding mortgage*, comply with it by forwarding the necessary funds to the mortgagee and on receipt from the mortgagee of the executed Form 53 forward it to the buyer's solicitor. The buyer's solicitor is usually asked to return written confirmation that the seller's solicitor is now discharged from their undertaking.
- If the seller has obtained *bridging finance* in connection with a related purchase, honour the undertaking given to the bank. (Be sure that you have first deducted all items which you are authorised to deduct, eg. your fees, estate agent's commission.)
- Pay any *balance in the proceeds of sale* to the seller or in accordance with their instructions.

12.5.2 Buyer's solicitor: stamping the transfer

If stamp duty is payable, the buyer's solicitor must, within 30 days, send the transfer to the Inland Revenue together with a client account cheque. At the same time a completed Particulars Delivered (PD) form must be submitted. When the transfer is returned by the Inland Revenue it will bear embossed stamps showing the amount of duty which has been paid and a printed stamp showing that particulars have been delivered. The Land Registry will not accept the transfer for registration until it has been stamped.

If there is no duty payable the PD form is not submitted to the Inland Revenue but is submitted instead to the Land Registry together with the application for registration.

Buyer's solicitor: registering the transfer 12.5.3

Within the 30 working day priority period granted by the Form 94A search, application must be made to the Land Registry to register the transfer. A late application will be subject to any new entries made since the date of the search. The application must therefore be lodged in time even if the documentation is incomplete, eg. if Form 53 has not yet been received from the seller's solicitor.

The application is made on Form A4 and in most residential transactions the application is to do three things:

- Remove the seller's *discharged mortgage(s)* from the Register;
- Register the buyer(s) as the new *proprietor(s)*;
- Register the new *charge(s)* created by the buyer.

The documents to be lodged with the A4 application will then be the:

- Charge certificate(s);
- Form 53 for each discharged mortgage;
- Form 19 Transfer;
- Original mortgage deed and certified copy for each new mortgage; and
- Fee.

Note

There is no fee for removing a charge. The fee for registering a transfer depends on the amount of the consideration. There is a fee for registering a charge but if it is done at the same time as a transfer is registered, the additional fee is waived.

Sometimes additional title documents will be required to link the information in the land/charge certificate with the transfer, eg. a copy of the death certificate of a deceased proprietor and, if a new trustee has been appointed, the deed of appointment.

Where there are joint buyers Form A4 asks whether or not the survivor can give a receipt for capital monies arising. If the answer is 'No', the appropriate co-ownership restriction will be entered in the Proprietorship Register.

If in the transfer the transferee has given an indemnity in respect of the transferor's continuing liability on covenants, the Land Registry will make a note of this personal covenant on the Proprietorship Register. This will remind the proprietor, when they come to sell, that they need to take an indemnity from the next buyer.

If the Land Registry has queries about the application it will raise requisitions and in disposing of the property the seller has guaranteed to assist in such matters (*see* Chapter 8, para. 8.6.1).

12.5.4 Custody of documents

Eventually a land or charge certificate will be received from the Land Registry. It should be checked to ensure it records accurately the name(s) and address(es) of the new proprietor(s) and all other necessary entries, eg. the new charge and any co-ownership restriction. The charge certificate should be sent to the mortgagee together with the bankruptcy search result and other important documents affecting the property such as the NHBC guarantee and planning consents.

If there is no mortgage the land certificate and all other documents will be sent to the buyer with advice as to their safekeeping.

Self-assessment questions

1 The buyer's solicitor tells you to go and do a completion. List three things you would expect to have to do.

2 What is the Law Society's code for completion by post?

3 In what circumstances can

(a) AV stamping, and

(b) PD stamping

be done at the Land Registry?

4 What is the effect of failing to register the transfer within 30 working days of the Form 94A search?

Chapter 13

Remedies

Delayed completion 13.1

If completion does not take place at the contractually agreed time, the party responsible for the delay will be liable for breach of contract. Although the other party will not normally be entitled to terminate the contract – as time is not generally of the essence of the contract – they will be entitled to compensation.

Note

Standard Condition 6.1.2 provides that if the money due on completion is received *after 2pm*, completion is regarded, for the purpose of calculating compensation, as taking place on the next working day. Thus, a liability for several days' interest will arise if completion was due to take place on the day before a bank holiday weekend.

The open contract approach 13.1.1

Regardless of who is responsible for the delay, the open contract rule seeks to put the parties in the position they would have been had completion taken place on time. The *seller* is entitled to receive interest at the contract rate on the outstanding purchase price and the *buyer* is entitled to receive any income accruing from the property and is liable for all outgoings.

If the *seller* is the defaulting party:

- They must pay the buyer a fair rent if they remain in occupation; (In practice this will normally cancel out the buyer's liability to pay interest.)
- The buyer is entitled to elect to allow the seller to retain the income from the property (and therefore not pay rent) instead of the buyer paying interest;
- The buyer is entitled to elect to place the outstanding purchase price on deposit and pay over to the seller the interest it actually earns instead of paying interest at the contract rate. This option will generally only be available to a cash buyer as if completion is delayed a buyer's mortgage funds will not be released and therefore will not be available to place on deposit.

If the *buyer* is the defaulting party, none of these options is open to the buyer.

In *addition* to these adjustments there can also be an

ordinary common law claim for damages to compensate whichever is the innocent party for any loss resulting from the breach of contract.

13.1.2 Damages

The normal rules regarding remoteness of damage apply and the plaintiff is entitled to compensation for those consequences of the breach that were reasonably foreseeable: *Hadley v Baxendale* (1854) and *The Heron II* (1969).

Example

In *Raineri v Miles* (1981), the defendant contracted to sell their house in West London to the plaintiff and to buy another house from a third party. Completion was fixed for 12 July on both contracts. Late on 11 July the third party informed the defendant that due to difficulties with the finance for their own purchase, they would not be able to complete the sale to the defendant the following day. The defendant immediately notified the plaintiff but they had already vacated their house in the north of England and their furniture was on its way south. The defendant did not vacate on the 12th and the plaintiff had to rent temporary accommodation. The defendant did, however, help the plaintiff to mitigate their loss by providing storage for the furniture. On 11 August the defendant was able to complete on their purchase and consequently on their sale to the plaintiff. The plaintiff sued for damages to cover their accommodation costs. The defendant settled the claim and sought indemnity from the third party. The main issue was whether the defendant had been in breach, given that their failure to complete on time was due to the default of the third party.

The House of Lords held that they were in breach and liable to the plaintiff and therefore entitled to be indemnified by the third party. A delay on one transaction is no excuse for failing to perform a related transaction on time.

Where it is the buyer who fails to complete on time a seller with a related purchase will be faced with either delaying their purchase or raising bridging finance to complete on time. Bridging finance is very expensive and therefore delaying the related purchase, even though it will involve liability to their seller, may be preferable.

Where the seller was planning to purchase with the aid of a mortgage, the mortgagee will not release the funds if their sale, and consequently the discharge of the mortgage on that property, is delayed. The seller would therefore need bridging finance to cover the delayed mortgage funds as well as the delayed proceeds of sale.

Note

There is always a duty on the innocent party to mitigate the loss.

The Standard Conditions 13.1.3

The sale contract usually modifies the open contract rules regarding the consequences of delay.

- *SC 6.3.2* provides that in a sale with vacant possession the apportionment of income and outgoings is to be made with effect from the date of actual completion and not the date when completion should have occurred.
- *SC 7.3.1* provides that it is the party in default who has to pay compensation/interest and not, as under the open contract, always the buyer.
- *SC 7.3.2* provides that the party whose period of default is the greater shall pay compensation calculated at the contract rate on the purchase price, or (where the buyer is the paying party) the purchase price less any deposit paid.
- *SC 7.3.3* makes it clear that a claim for damages for breach of contract can still be brought if the loss exceeds the fixed compensation provided for in SC 7.3.2.

Notice to complete 13.1.4

A notice to complete is a device for making *time of the essence*, ie. making the time for completion a condition of the contract. It sets a deadline and if completion does not take place by that date, the party who is *then* responsible for the failure to complete has committed a major breach, ie. a breach of condition. The other party may then elect to withdraw from the contract and in addition claim damages for non-completion. This threat to terminate the contract if completion does not take place by the deadline may well induce a dilatory party to complete.

Under the *open contract rule* a notice to complete can be served at any time *after* the contractual completion date and completion must then be within the specified time or if no time is specified within a reasonable time.

Special Condition 6.8 provides that a notice to complete can be given at any time *on or after* the completion date and that completion must then be within 10 working days. The party giving the notice must be ready, able and willing to complete. The notice makes time of the essence for *both* parties so that if the party serving the notice is later responsible for completion not taking place by the deadline, the party on whom the notice was served will then be the one entitled to terminate the contract and claim damages.

Note

SC 6.8.4 seeks to ensure that if the buyer fails to comply with a completion notice, the seller will have in hand the traditional 10% deposit which can then be forfeited.

If completion does not take place by the deadline the *innocent party* may:

- *Terminate* the contract and *claim damages* for non-performance;
- *Waive* the deadline and allow the other side extra time. If it is later decided to impose a further deadline, another notice to complete will be needed;
- Sue for *specific performance.*

13.1.5 Specific performance

A decree of specific performance can be applied for even before the contractual date for completion if there is reason to believe that the other party will not perform, but it is normally only sought after there has been some delay. Often a notice to complete is tried first and only if that fails to induce completion is specific performance sought.

Specific performance is primarily a buyer's remedy but a seller may seek it where it is believed that the buyer has the money to complete but is refusing to do so. It is an equitable, and therefore a *discretionary* remedy, and may be refused if, for example, the court considers that to award it would cause undue hardship to the defendant. Damages may be awarded in lieu of specific performance. If a decree of specific performance is not complied with, the plaintiff may ask the court to terminate the contract and award damages instead: *Johnson v Agnew* (1980).

13.2 Non-completion

A failure to complete will constitute a major breach and entitle the other party to terminate the contract where:

- There is a failure to complete on time and *time is of the essence*, either because it was made so originally or because a notice to complete has been served;
- The seller is *unable to transfer what they contracted to transfer*. This may be because they cannot show a good title, or because there was some major misdescription in the contract or the non-disclosure of some major incumbrance. (Where title is investigated pre-exchange there is less chance of this type of problem arising.)

  The buyer can immediately terminate the contract and

does not first have to serve a notice to complete, although in practice the buyer may allow the seller time to try to remedy the defect. If the buyer elects to complete despite the defect, they will be entitled to damages for the diminution in the value of the property and will therefore be entitled to a price reduction.

Where the contract is terminated both parties are discharged from further performance and the innocent party can also claim damages for non-performance.

Damages recoverable by a buyer 13.2.1

The normal rules of remoteness apply and the buyer can recover for the reasonably foreseeable consequences of the breach.

- A loss of a bargain is foreseeable, so in a rising market the buyer will recover the difference between the contract price and the increased value of the property.
- Wasted conveyancing costs are not recoverable as these would have been incurred anyway to acquire the bargain.

Note

If there is no claim for loss of bargain, wasted costs can be claimed.

- A claim for loss of profit, eg. on reselling or on developing the property, will only succeed if the seller knew of the buyer's intention to resell/develop.
- In a chain transaction a breach by a seller will probably result in the buyer breaking their related sale contract and incurring liability, at least for delay, to their buyer. This can normally be recovered, as in residential conveyancing the existence of a related transaction is generally known to all parties and the loss is therefore foreseeable.

  If the buyer completes, whether on time or belatedly, on their related sale they will need temporary accommodation until they can find another house to buy. The cost of this and the costs of the new purchase are recoverable: *Beard v Porter* (1948).

The buyer will also be entitled to the return of the deposit plus interest. SC 7.6.2 confirms this and SC 7.6.3 leaves untouched the common law claim for damages for breach.

Damages recoverable by a seller 13.2.2

Where non-completion is due to the buyer's default the

seller is entitled to retain the deposit and accrued interest irrespective of whether or not the seller has suffered any loss. The court does have a discretion under s.49(2), LPA 1925 to order its return but this is most unlikely to be exercised if the deposit is the traditional 10%.

If the seller claims damages the forfeited deposit must be brought into account. It is therefore only where the seller's loss exceeds the amount of the deposit that the seller will need to claim damages.

- In a falling market the seller's loss of bargain will be the difference between the contract price and the decreased market value, which will be taken to be the price achieved on a resale provided it occurs within a reasonable time.
- Wasted conveyancing costs are not recoverable but the costs of the resale are.

Note

Wasted costs are recoverable if the seller does not claim for loss of bargain but then the deposit cannot be forfeited so such a claim is most unlikely.

- Where the seller has a related purchase, and the buyer knows this, then liability incurred to that seller will also be recoverable.

13.2.3 The date for assessing damages

As a general rule damages for breach of contract are assessed as at the date of breach and then carry interest from that date. In a number of conveyancing cases it has been recognised that this is not always appropriate.

Example

In *Wroth v Tyler* (1974), where specific performance was sought but the court awarded damages in lieu, the plaintiff was awarded the difference between the contract price of £6,000 and the market value at the date of judgment, which was £11,500.

In *Johnson v Agnew* (1980) specific performance was ordered but subsequently became impossible because the mortgagee took possession and sold the property. The buyer therefore asked for damages instead and the date on which the mortgagee contracted to sell was taken as the appropriate date. The House of Lords held that the general rule that damages should be assessed at the date of breach is not an inflexible rule and that the court has power to select such other date as is appropriate to avoid injustice to the innocent party.

Misrepresentation 13.3

A misrepresentation in the negotiations leading to the contract will, if it induces the contract, render it voidable (*see* Chapter 9, para. 9.4). The fact that the misrepresentation may have become a term of the contract, or that the contract may have been performed by completion taking place, does not prevent the party misled seeking rescission: s.1, Misrepresentation Act 1967. Remember, however, that:

- Rescission is an equitable and therefore a discretionary remedy;
- It depends on restitution of the parties to their pre-contract position being possible – if completion has taken place this may not be possible;
- Section 2(2), Misrepresentation Act 1967 provides that if the misrepresentation was not fraudulent, the court may refuse rescission and award damages in lieu.

If the misrepresentation was not fraudulent the court may refuse rescission and award damages in lieu: s.2(2), Misrepresentation Act 1967. A claim for damages may be brought under s.2(1) but will fail if the defendant can prove that they had reasonable grounds to believe and did believe up to the time the contract was made that the facts represented were true.

Section 3 provides that a contractual term which seeks to exclude or restrict liability for, or the remedies for, misrepresentation shall be ineffective unless it is reasonable. Under s.11(1), Unfair Contract Terms Act 1977 the term must be fair and reasonable having regard to the circumstances which were, or ought reasonably to have been, known to or in the contemplation of the parties when the contract was made. SC 7.1.3 does seek to restrict the circumstances in which rescission can be obtained for negligent or innocent misrepresentation by providing that rescission is only possible where the property differs substantially from what the injured party had been led to expect. Its reasonableness has not been tested but it is probably acceptable.

Note

SC 7.1.3 also applies to misdescription and non-disclosure. These constitute a breach of contract which, if sufficiently serious, will entitle the innocent party to rescind, not in the sense of seeking restoration to the pre-contract position as in the case of misrepresentation, but in the sense of terminating/repudiating the contract for the future. It could be argued that if a misdescription or non-disclosure is fraudulent or reckless then, regardless of its seriousness, SC 7.1.3 makes termination possible, but this is almost certainly not so.

13.4 Post-completion

13.4.1 The doctrine of merger

At completion, or possibly at registration in the case of registered titles, the contract merges in the transfer, ie. the contract is terminated to the extent that it is intended to be performed by the transfer. Consequently, an action for breach of contract cannot generally be brought post-completion. Terms of the contract which are not performed by the transfer remain outstanding and can still be sued on, eg. a term that vacant possession will be given or a term that the seller will carry out certain repairs to the property. SC 7.4 confirms this.

It is generally believed that damages for late completion can still be claimed and there is also a long-standing rule that an express contractual term providing for damages for misdescription survives: *Palmer v Johnson* (1884). SC 7.1.2 is such an express term.

If, therefore, a material misdescription of the property only comes to light after completion, the buyer can still claim damages for breach of contract, but the same would not apply to a non-disclosure.

The merger rule only affects actions based on the contract and does not prevent actions on other grounds. Rescission for misrepresentation can still be claimed post-completion by virtue of s.1, Misrepresentation Act 1967, as can damages under s.2(1). The restriction on rescission contained in SC 7.1.3, assuming it is reasonable, probably also survives, as it would be anomalous for it to operate to restrict a buyer's right to rescind pre-completion but not post-completion.

13.4.2 The covenants for title

Depending on the type of title guarantee given in the transfer, the seller will have given certain implied covenants for title (*see* Chapter 8, para 8.6). The seller's potential liability on these covenants will last for 12 years from the date of the transfer. The benefit of the covenants will run with the estate transferred and they can therefore be enforced by later estate owners.

Even where full title guarantee has been given, the seller will not be liable for loss caused by:

- *Charges and other interests* appearing in the Register at the time of the transfer;
- Any *overriding interest* of which the purchaser has notice;
- Any other matter to which the disposition was *expressly made subject*;

- Any further matter which was either within the *actual knowledge* of the purchaser or was a *necessary consequence of facts* that were within their actual knowledge.

Once a disposition has been registered, the only covenants of any importance to the buyer are likely to be those concerning third party rights. Where, however, the buyer fails to register the transfer within the priority period of their search, the court might consider that their failure was the course of their loss and they might therefore be unable to recover from the seller.

Note

Implied covenants for title are also given in mortgages, leases and assignments of leases and may therefore provide remedies to mortgagees, original lessees and assignees of leases.

Where the seller has given only limited title guarantee and an incumbrance comes to light after completion, the seller will not be liable if it was created by a previous owner from whom the seller acquired the property. The buyer may, however, be able to claim against the previous seller because the benefit of the implied covenant which they gave when selling runs with the land, but they may not be traceable.

The implied covenants do not provide a remedy for all post-completion problems. However, action on them has occasionally succeeded in the past. The introduction of the new covenants may generate more claims in future, at least until issues such as what the person making the disposition can 'reasonably be expected to know about' (s.3(1), Law of Property (Miscellaneous Provisions) Act 1994) are clarified.

Example

In *Dunning & Sons Ltd v Sykes & Son Ltd* (1987), on a sale of part of the land comprised in the seller's title, the plan in the transfer included a small area of land which was no longer part of the seller's title as it had been the subject of a previous sale. There was therefore a discrepancy between the transfer plan and the verbal description of the property which referred to the Register and consequently to a smaller area. The Court of Appeal held that the transfer plan should prevail as 'where parcels in a conveyancing document are described by reference to a plan attached to the document, the natural inference is that it was the intention that anyone concerned should see from the document alone, which means from the plan on it, what land the document was purporting to pass'. The seller was therefore held to be in breach of the implied covenant for title.

Self-assessment questions

1 What is the effect of either party being unable to complete on the contractually agreed date?

2 What is a notice to complete?

3 Why do sellers rarely need to sue buyers for damages for failure to complete?

4 When the seller is unable to transfer what they contracted to sell can the buyer:

(a) Withdraw from the contract?

(b) Recover their deposit?

(c) Recover their wasted conveyancing costs?

(d) Recover by way of damages an increase in the value of the property?

(e) Recover the cost of buying another property?

(f) Recover any damages they might have to pay to their buyer if they delay completing on their related sale?

(g) Recover accommodation and storage costs if they complete on a related sale and are therefore homeless?

(h) Recover the deposit which they had paid, and have now lost, on a new kitchen which they had ordered for their new home?

Chapter 14

Unregistered freeholds: deducing and investigating title

Deducing title 14.1

Where the title is unregistered there is no register you can consult to see who is the owner of the estate. Instead, ownership must be proved by tracing a chain of title back through the title deeds to a *good root of title*. The open contract rules require that this root be at least 15 years old.

Note

All references in this chapter are to the Law of Property Act 1925 unless otherwise stated.

A good root of title 14.1.1

There is no statutory definition of a good root of title but it is generally accepted that it must be a document which:

- Deals with the *whole estate* which is the subject of the sale;
- Contains an *adequate description* of the property;
- Contains *nothing to cast doubt* on the title.

Deals with the whole estate

This means that if you are dealing with the freehold title a document which deals only with the leasehold title or only with the beneficial interest will not be good enough. However, it does not mean that the root document cannot include other land which is not the subject of the sale.

Example

The present seller may have bought the land within the last 15 years from someone who did not part with the whole of the property. To deduce title back for a sufficient period, the seller will have to trace title to a document which comprised more than is currently being sold.

Nor does it mean that there can be only one root of title.

Example

What is now being sold may in the past have consisted of two pieces of land which, within the last 15 years, came into common ownership. The present seller will therefore have to trace title back to two roots of title.

The description of the property

Ideally, this should be a freestanding description which does not require reference to any other document. However, a root which describes the property by reference to a description in an earlier document will be acceptable if that earlier document is also provided.

Does not cast doubt on the title

The fact that the root refers to certain earlier incumbrances which affect the property does not cast doubt on the title, although details of those earlier incumbrances, eg. covenants, will have to be supplied with the root document.

What would cast doubt on the title would be if the root document said, for example, that the then seller could not prove title but only had title by adverse possession.

Acceptable roots

The most acceptable root of title is a *conveyance on sale*. A voluntary conveyance, ie. a conveyance by way of gift, or an assent by personal representatives to a beneficiary, may meet the three characteristics specified for a good root but will not be as acceptable as a conveyance on sale because a donee or assentee will not have investigated the title, whereas on a sale, the then buyer would have investigated their seller's title back for a further period of at least 15 years.

A mortgage is technically not a good root because it does not deal with the entire estate as the mortgagor retains the freehold title. It may, however, be used where you can be certain that the mortgagee would have investigated the title back for at least a further 15 years. This the mortgagee would have done if they were an institutional mortgagee and the mortgage was for a large amount relative to the value of the property, but this is probably impossible to ascertain. It will therefore only be used as the root of title if there is nothing better available.

14.1.2 The age of the root

The 15-year rule

Under the open contract rule as laid down in s.44 (as amended by s.23, LPA 1969) the root of title must be at least 15 years old, but to find a document which satisfies this requirement it may be necessary to go back *much further* than 15 years.

Note

The open contract rule is not normally modified by the terms of the contract. It would be most exceptional to find a buyer insisting on an older root of title.

Shorter roots

Sometimes the seller offers the buyer a shorter, ie. a younger, root. There are *specific risks* for a buyer in accepting a shorter root.

- The buyer will be fixed with *constructive notice of any incumbrances* that would have been discovered had title been investigated for the normal statutory period.

  This means that if an investigation back to a good root at least 15 years old would have revealed certain third party rights, and if the enforceability of those rights depends on the doctrine of notice, eg. pre-1926 restrictive covenants, then the buyer will `be bound by them.
- The buyer will not be entitled to compensation under s.25, LPA 1969 in respect of registered land charges which would have been discoverable had title been investigated for the normal statutory period.

Registered land charges

The weakness of the system of registration of land charges under the Land Charges Acts 1925 and 1972 is that charges are registered against the names of previous estate owners. A buyer therefore needs to know the names of previous estate owners to search against.

An investigation of title will reveal the names of previous estate owners back to the root of title and the buyer will therefore be able to make a land charges search against those names.

If land charges are registered against the names of pre-root estate owners the buyer will still be bound by those charges, but s.25, LPA 1969 provides for compensation to be paid to the buyer in these circumstances (*see* Chapter 17, para. 17.3.1). This compensation will *not* be available, however, where the buyer's failure to discover a registered land charge was because they accepted a root less than 15 years old and not because the charge was registered against a name hidden behind the normal minimum 15-year root.

Note

The non-availability of compensation under s.25 is more serious for a buyer than being fixed with constructive notice as there are many more third party rights whose enforceability depends on registration than there are third party rights whose enforceability depends on the old doctrine of notice.

The abstract of title 14.1.3

The chain of title from the root document to the present day is set out chronologically in an abstract of title.

The traditional abstract of title consisted of a précis of the contents of the title deeds. Nowadays what is usually provided is a schedule, called an epitome, setting out in chronological order the documents and events constituting the chain of title together with photocopies of the relevant documents.

Note

The term 'abstract' is often used to encompass both the traditional abstract and the more modern epitome plus copy documents and it will be used to cover both from now on.

At some stage, probably not until completion, the buyer will need to check the abstract against the original deeds to ensure its accuracy and to ensure that their investigation of title has therefore been based on accurate information.

14.1.4 Documents to be abstracted

The abstract will commence with the *root of title.*

This will be followed by any *pre-root documents*, or extracts from them, which need to be included.

Example

1 If the root describes the property by reference to a description and/or plan in an *earlier document*, that earlier description and/or plan must be abstracted.

2 If the root refers to earlier covenants or easements, or if at the time of the root transaction there was a prior undischarged mortgage, the details of these *outstanding incumbrances* must be included.

3 If the root document was executed pursuant to a previously granted power of attorney then the *power of attorney* must also be abstracted.

There will then follow in chronological order the documents which form the *links in the chain of title* from the root to the present day, eg. conveyances, grants of representation, assents and mortgages (including the present seller's mortgage(s), which will be discharged on completion).

Note

A legal mortgage is an essential link in the chain of title and even discharged mortgages must be abstracted. Thus, the abstract will show that at a certain date a mortgage was granted and then show that at a later date it was discharged.

Leases which have expired by passage of time do not need to be included but leases which have come to an end in other ways, eg. by surrender or forfeiture, must be abstracted.

Death (and *marriage*) *certificates* are documents of record and copies of them could be obtained by the buyer if they are given the relevant dates, but in practice sellers usually provide copies of any necessary certificates.

Central land charges certificates obtained on the occasion of previous transactions relating to the property are generally kept with the title deeds. Although they are not title documents, and therefore do not have to be included in the abstract, sellers, as a matter of courtesy, will generally include any certificates that they have. This may mean that pre-completion the buyer will not need to do their own search against names in respect of which the seller has supplied search certificates.

Investigation of title 14.2

The buyer will investigate the seller's title by:

- Examining the abstract of title;
- Carrying out certain pre-completion searches (*see* Chapter 16, para. 16.4);
- Verifying the title by checking the abstract against the original deeds (*see* Chapter 17, para. 17.1.1).

Examining the abstract 14.2.1

The buyer must investigate the *chain of title* by checking that all the documents in the chain:

- Are *properly executed*;
- Are *properly stamped* (if they require stamping); and
- Form an *unbroken chain of title*, ie. the buyer must check for any missing or weak links in the chain. If any are found corrective action will be necessary. This can be a complex business, if previous conveyancing transactions have not been carried out as carefully as they should have been.

Stamping 14.2.2

It is the *seller's responsibility* to ensure that all title documents which required stamping at the time of their execution are properly stamped and the seller cannot contract out of this obligation.

An unstamped or incorrectly stamped document is *not admissible* in evidence. It will *not* constitute a good root or link in a chain of title and will *not be accepted* by the Land Registry on any application for registration.

Late stamping may involve the seller in payment of a penalty to the Inland Revenue.

Note

In the past many conveyancing documents attracted stamp duty but over the years stamping requirements have been reduced. It is beyond the scope of this companion to give details of these old stamp duties but remember that if you encounter a mortgage, or mortgage discharge, dated prior to 1 August 1971 it may have been subject to stamp duty. Also an assent, a deed of appointment of a new trustee or a power of attorney executed before 26 March 1985 should have been stamped with a fixed rate duty of 50p and a voluntary transfer, ie. deed of gift, prior to that date would have required *ad valorem* stamp duty to be paid on the value of the gift.

14.2.3 Requisitions on title

The buyer is entitled to raise queries on the title (*requisitions*) to ensure that they have full details of the title and of any incumbrances affecting it. If any defects in the title are discovered the seller will be required to rectify them. If they cannot be rectified and consequently the seller cannot prove a good title to the property, the buyer will be entitled not to proceed.

Barring requisitions

Section 45 provides that the buyer is not entitled to raise requisitions on pre-root root matters. There are, however, important *exceptions* to this rule and the buyer is entitled to require the seller to produce:

- Any *power of attorney* under which an abstracted document is executed;
- Any document creating or disposing of an *incumbrance* which still affected the property at the time of the root conveyance;
- Any *plan* referred to in the root document.

Requisitions may also be barred by *special conditions* in the contract. Where any aspect of the title has been shown to the buyer before contracts are exchanged, it is usual for the contract to provide that after exchange the buyer will not raise any requisitions on that matter, eg. if details of restrictive covenants binding the property have been fully disclosed in the draft contract. Where the *Protocol* is being followed and the entire title is deduced pre-exchange, a special condition should bar all requisitions post-exchange.

Sale by a sole seller 14.3

Where the title is owned by just one person the conveyance by them alone will give the buyer legal title. However, if there is anyone else with a beneficial interest in the property the buyer will be bound by that interest if the buyer has notice of it and the buyer will be fixed with constructive notice of the beneficiary's right if the beneficiary is in occupation and their right could reasonably have been discovered from inspection of the property (the rule in *Hunt v Luck* (1902) and s.199).

Where such a beneficial interest exists, the buyer must insist on the seller appointing a second trustee so that the buyer can pay the purchase money to at least two trustees and so overreach the beneficiary's interest.

Sale by a surviving co-owner 14.4

Where the title was owned by two or more persons but the others have died and there is now only one surviving co-owner, the survivor will by virtue of the *right of survivorship* have sole legal title.

Whether or not the buyer's solicitor should insist on the survivor appointing a second trustee depends on how the beneficial title was held. You must first look at the conveyance to the co-owners. This may specify how they held the beneficial title. If it says that they held for themselves as beneficial *joint tenants*, then provided that the joint tenancy was not severed before the first one died, the survivor will also have sole beneficial title and it will not be necessary to insist on the appointment of a second trustee.

The problem is: how can you be sure that the beneficial joint tenancy has not been severed? The Law of Property (Joint Tenants) Act 1964 was specifically designed to protect a purchaser in this situation. It provides that a purchaser is entitled to assume that the joint tenancy has not, at the time of death, been severed if:

- There is *no memorandum of severance* endorsed on the conveyance to the joint tenants;
- There is no *bankruptcy entry* recorded at the Land Charges Registry against the names of either of the joint tenants;
- The conveyance contains a statement that the survivor is *solely and beneficially interested*.

The buyer from a sole surviving co-owner must therefore:

- Have proof of death of any co-owners;
- Check the *conveyance* to the co-owners to ensure that

they held initially as beneficial joint tenants;

- Check that there is no *memorandum of severance* endorsed on that conveyance;
- Undertake a *bankruptcy search* against the names of the joint tenants; and
- Ensure that the conveyance states that the survivor is *solely and beneficially entitled*.

Note

Prior to the Law of Property (Miscellaneous Provisions) Act 1994 the survivor could alternatively have conveyed as beneficial owner. Therefore, when examining a title which includes an earlier disposition by a surviving co-owner you should expect to find them conveying as beneficial owner rather than stating that they were solely and beneficially interested.

The buyer should insist on the appointment of a second trustee if:

- The requirements of the 1964 Act are not satisfied;
- The conveyance to the co-owners states that they held as beneficial tenants in common or does not state how they held beneficially;
- If there is any reason to suppose that they were holding not simply on trust for themselves but on trust for some other third party.

14.5 Sale by a mortgagee

There is no fundamental difference between a mortgagee's sale of a registered title and of an unregistered title. The existence of the power of sale, when it arises, when it becomes exercisable and the effect of its exercise are all exactly the same.

14.5.1 Second mortgages

Where there is more than one mortgage on the property the second mortgagee will probably (invariably in the case of an institutional mortgagee) have notified the first mortgagee of their existence. Nevertheless, a first mortgagee selling should always search the Land Charges Register to see if there is a second mortgagee to whom any surplus in the proceeds of sale should be handed. If they fail to do so and hand the surplus back to the mortgagor, they will be liable to the second mortgagee to the extent of the latter's interest.

14.5.2 Equitable mortgages

An equitable mortgage of an unregistered title can be

created by the deposit of title deeds with the creditor together with a contract, which must comply with s.2, Law of Property (Miscellaneous Provisions) Act 1989, to create a legal mortgage if required to do so.

If this contact (usually referred to as a *memorandum of deposit*) goes beyond the requirements of s.2 and is by deed, the equitable mortgagee will have a statutory power of sale but will not be able to convey the mortgagor's legal title to a buyer unless the mortgage deed contains either:

- A *trust clause* whereby the mortgagor acknowledges that they hold the legal title on trust for the mortgagee and will convey it in accordance with the direction of the mortgagee when required to do so; or
- An *irrevocable power of attorney clause* (*see* Chapter 18, para. 18.2.8) which would enable the mortgagee to convey the mortgagor's legal title as their agent.

Third party rights 14.6

Appropriate action must be taken when third party rights are encountered.

Mortgages 14.6.1

Discharge

A mortgage can be discharged by the seller redeeming it, ie. paying it off. A separate deed of discharge could be executed but this is not normally done as s.115 provides that a receipt which names the payer and is endorsed on the mortgage deed is equally effective. Such a receipt is known as a *statutory receipt*.

Note

Where the mortgagee is a building society, there is an alternative form of receipt which does not specify the name of the payer.

As with registered titles the discharge of the seller's mortgage may not actually take place prior to completion. The seller's solicitor may give an undertaking to forward the money to the mortgagee to discharge the mortgage and then to forward, when received from the mortgagee, the discharged mortgage deed.

Note

Where the mortgage is discharged pursuant to such an undertaking, it is important that the receipt on the mortgage deed should be dated on or before the date of the conveyance to the buyer so that events appear to have taken place in the correct sequence, ie. the seller's mortgage is discharged before the conveyance by the seller to the buyer.

Second mortgages

Where a second mortgage on the property is discharged, any C(i) land charge lodged to protect it is now redundant and the buyer will take free from it but they should still require the seller to secure the charge's removal from the Register or to hand over at completion an application for its removal signed by the second mortgagee. This is to ensure that the Land Charges Register is not cluttered with obsolete entries.

14.6.2 Beneficial interests

The position for unregistered titles is the same as that described in Chapter 7, para. 7.6.2 for registered titles.

14.6.3 MHA rights

A spouse's right of occupation under the Matrimonial Homes Act 1983 is registrable as a Class F land charge. If so protected the buyer will take subject to it. The only way that it can be removed is by the spouse who entered it applying to the Land Charges Department for its removal.

The position is therefore very similar to that described in Chapter 7, para. 7.6.3 and the buyer must not complete unless the Class F charge has already been removed or the buyer receives an application for its removal signed by the spouse.

14.6.4 Covenants and easements

The position is the same as that described in Chapter 7, para. 7.6.4.

14.6.5 Estate contracts

These are registrable as Class C(iv) land charges and the position is the same as in Chapter 7, para. 7.6.4.

14.6.6 Local land charges

The position is exactly the same as in Chapter 7, para. 7.6.6.

Self-assessment questions

1 What is the difference between a root of title and chain of title?

2 Why is a conveyance on sale the best root of title?

3 A buyer from a surviving co-owner will need to examine the conveyance to the seller and the deceased. What two things will the buyer particularly look for?

4 Which of the following must be included in an abstract of title?

(a) Pre-root documents.

(b) Discharged mortgages.

(c) Expired leases.

(d) Old land charge certificates.

(e) Death certificates.

(f) The seller's mortgage which will be redeemed at completion and will not therefore bind the buyer.

Chapter 15

Unregistered freeholds: pre-exchange

Taking instructions 15.1

The main difference from taking instructions for the sale of a registered title (*see* Chapter 3) is that you need to obtain the *title deeds* instead of the land/charge certificate. If the property is *mortgaged* the mortgagee will have the deeds. As there is only one set of title deeds they will be with the first mortgagee and any later mortgagee should have registered their mortgage as a C(i) land charge (*puisne* mortgage) at the Land Charges Department at Plymouth.

You will write to the mortgagee requesting the title deeds, giving the usual undertaking for their safekeeping and return.

Drafting the contract 15.2

Before drafting the contract you must investigate the seller's title to:

- Ensure that the seller can *prove title*; and to
- Discover if there are any *incumbrances* which will bind a buyer and which therefore need to be disclosed in the draft contract.

The main *differences* between a contract for the sale of a registered freehold (*see* Chapter 8) and an unregistered freehold will be the:

- *Description* of the property (the particulars of sale);
- Need to specify a *root of title*;
- *Incumbrances* subject to which the property is sold.

The particulars of sale 15.2.1

This is the description of the property being sold. It may be a freestanding description which does not refer to any other document, for example:

The property known as 22 Station Road, Melbury, Northshire having a frontage to Station Road of 12 metres and a depth from Station Road of 30 metres on the western boundary and 32 metres on the eastern boundary.

Alternatively it may describe the property by reference to the subject matter of an earlier conveyance, for example:

The property known as 22 Station Road, Melbury, Northshire being the property comprised in a conveyance dated 2 May 1970 between Jessica Evans (1) and Jeremy Hobbs and Elizabeth Hobbs (2).

The deed referred to in this second method will often be the holding deed, ie. the deed under which the seller obtained title. However, if that deed does not itself contain a free-standing description of the property but refers back to a description in an earlier deed, the earlier deed will have to be referred to.

Whenever the property is described by reference to a description in another document, that other document, or at least an extract from it containing the description of what was conveyed, must be supplied with the draft contract.

Note

Reference back to a description in the holding deed, or an earlier deed, should ensure that the seller does not contract to sell more than they actually own, but you should always check whether they have previously sold off some of what was conveyed to them, or whether they have subsequently acquired extra land which they now intend to sell.

A *plan* is not essential where the seller is selling the whole of the land. If a plan is used it should be carefully drawn to scale and of sufficient size to be of use. (Poorly drawn plans are a major problem in the conveyancing of unregistered titles.)

If there is a conflict between the verbal description of the property and the plan (in a contract or in a conveyance) the question of which should prevail will arise. If the property is stated to be 'more particularly delineated on the plan' then the plan prevails. If the plan is said to be 'for the purpose of identification only', then the verbal description will prevail. This does not mean that the plan can be ignored as it may supplement the verbal description. It is only if there is a conflict between the two that the words will prevail.

15.2.2 The root of title

The open contract rule requires the root of title to be at least *15 years old* and the contract does not generally vary this. If the seller does offer a shorter title, ie. a root of title which is less than 15 years old, there will be risks for the buyer if they accept it. (*See* Chapter 14, para. 14.1.2.)

The contract must specify what instrument is being offered as the root of title and state its date and the names of the parties. Generally the root offered will be a conveyance on sale. A copy of this document does not have to be provided with the contract unless:

- It contains the *description* of the property; or
- It contains *details of incumbrances* subject to which the property is sold (*see* below); or
- *Title is being fully deduced pre-exchange* (in which case a special condition should bar requisitions after exchange).

Incumbrances 15.2.3

Incumbrances subject to which the property is sold must be specified either on the front of the contract form or in special conditions, for example:

The property is sold subject to the covenants contained in a conveyance dated 24 September 1960 between Algernon Brian Baron and Christopher Edward Lloyd (1) and Jessica Evans (2).

A copy of these covenants must then be supplied with the draft contract. The special condition will normally go on to provide that the buyer will raise no requisitions on them, which means that all enquiries on the covenants must be raised by the buyer before contracts are exchanged.

Pre-contract searches and enquiries 15.3

Most of the pre-contract searches and enquiries will be exactly the same as for a registered title (*see* Chapter 9). The *buyer's solicitor* needs to ensure that all necessary searches and enquiries are made and that the results and replies are satisfactory before the buyer exchanges contracts.

Thus, the buyer's solicitor must make:

- A *local land charges search;*
- *Enquiries* of the local authority;
- *Special searches and enquiries* as appropriate;
- *Pre-contract enquiries* of the seller if the seller does not provide a property information form.

They should also ensure that the buyer arranges a survey of the property to reveal its physical state.

Inspection of the property 15.3.1

The property must be inspected to:

- Check on what *fixtures* there are;
- Reveal any *patent incumbrances* which the seller is not obliged to disclose, eg. rights of way;
- Check on who is in *occupation* in case they have rights in respect of the property.

Rights of persons in occupation

In the case of both registered and unregistered titles an

inspection to discover whether there are occupiers needs to be made but the rights of any occupiers are protected differently under the two systems.

(a) *Registered titles.* If those in occupation (or in receipt of the rents or profits) at the time of the transfer have rights, those rights (with a few exceptions) will be protected as overriding interests under s.70(1)(g), LRA 1925.

(b) *Unregistered titles.* The inspection is to discover if there is anyone with rights, the enforceability of which depends on the *doctrine of notice.* The purchaser will be fixed with *constructive* notice of such rights if they would have come to the purchaser's knowledge if such enquiries and inspections had been made as ought reasonably to have been made: the rule in *Hunt v Luck* (1902) and s.199, LPA 1925. If the rights of the occupier were capable of registration under the Land Charges Act but they have not been registered, they will be void against the purchaser and notice is then irrelevant: *Midland Bank Trust Co v Greene* (1981).

Under *s.70(1)(g)* the key to the protection afforded is *occupation*. Under the rule in *Hunt v Luck* the key to the protection is that the right is *reasonably discoverable from inspection.*

The differences between the forms of protection

Section 70(1)(g) *Registered titles*	*The rule in Hunt and Luck* *Unregistered titles*
The occupier must be in occupation at completion.	Not applicable.
Occupation includes the receipt of rents and profits.	Not applicable.
Whatever rights in the land the occupier has will be protected, except MHA rights and rights of beneficiaries under a strict settlement.	Only rights whose enforceability depends on the doctrine of notice are protected, eg. the rights of beneficiaries and rights acquired by virtue of the doctrine of promissory estoppel.
Neither the occupation nor the occupier's right need be reasonably discoverable.	The buyer is only fixed with notice of rights that are reasonably discoverable from inspection of the property.

15.3.2 Index map search

This is an extra search which must be made whenever the title is unregistered. It is made at the appropriate district land registry but it is not a search of the Register but of a separate index which the Land Registry keeps based on the Ordnance Survey maps. The search is made on Form 96 and the result will show whether any:

- *Title is registered* in a particular piece of land and if so the title number;
- *Caution* against first registration has been lodged.

Note

A caution against first registration must not be confused with a caution against dealing. The latter is lodged where title is already registered in order to protect a minor interest which cannot be protected in any other way.

A caution against first registration is lodged where title is still unregistered. It entitles the cautioner to be notified whenever there is an application for first registration of title in that particular piece of land. The cautioner can then assert their claim to the land. They may be able to prevent its registration or limit the area of land included in the title or have the title registered subject to their right in the property.

Note

The index map search is the means by which any member of the public can discover the title number of a particular title and then apply for office copies of that title.

Land charges search: unregistered titles 15.3.3

A land charges search in the Central Register of Land Charges is primarily a pre-completion search (*see* Chapter 16, para. 16.4.1).

If title is not deduced pre-exchange, the buyer will not know the names of all previous estate owners to search against, but a search could be made against the seller's name. This should certainly be done in the case of a sole seller if there is any possibility of a spouse having registered a *Matrimonial Homes Act (Class F) charge,* or if there is reason to suspect that the seller may have created other charges, eg. other contracts affecting the land. The search will, however, need to be repeated pre-completion in order to obtain the benefit of the priority period.

Note

If title is deduced pre-exchange, a full search will be undertaken at this stage.

Deducing and investigating title 15.4

Where the Protocol is not adopted the abstract may be supplied and requisitions raised *after* exchange. This is the traditional procedure envisaged by SC 4.1.

The process of deducing and investigating title is more complex when the title is unregistered than when it is registered and there is a greater likelihood of requisitions being raised. If it is not done until after exchange and problems are then discovered, it may take time to sort them out and completion may be delayed as a result. The problem might even entitle the buyer to withdraw from the contract. It therefore makes practical sense, and is increasingly common, for title to be deduced pre-exchange – but it is not always done. On a complex title, such as the sale of a farm, the seller's solicitor may not be prepared to send the buyer a large bundle of copy documents and deal with all the requisitions until they are certain that the buyer is committed to proceeding with the purchase.

Note

As buyer's solicitor you should bear in mind that post-completion you will have to apply for first registration of title and that in order to obtain absolute title you will need to prove title to the satisfaction of the Land Registry. You must therefore be absolutely certain that all possible problems regarding the title are resolved.

15.5 Exchange of contracts

There is no difference between registered and unregistered titles (*see* Chapter 10).

Self-assessment questions

1 Are there any advantages/disadvantages in the contract describing the property to be sold by reference to the subject matter of an earlier conveyance?
2 Why should the contract never say that the property is 'for the purpose of identification only more particularly delineated on the attached plan'?
3 When will a buyer of an unregistered title be bound by the rights of those in occupation?
4 What is the difference between a caution against first registration and a caution against dealing and where is each one found?

Chapter 16

Unregistered freeholds: exchange to completion

The effect of a binding contract 16.1

The only difference here between registered and unregistered conveyancing is the mechanism for protecting the buyer's estate contract. It is registrable against the name of the seller as a Class C(iv) land charge in the Register of Land Charges at Plymouth.

Requisitions on title 16.2

The position is the same as that described in Chapter 11, para. 11.2.

Preparing the documentation 16.3

Here there is a major difference between registered and unregistered conveyancing. Unregistered titles are conveyed by a *deed of conveyance*.

There is no prescribed form to be completed but there is an established structure for a deed of conveyance which must be followed.

Deed of conveyance 16.3.1

Commencement and date
This identifies the document as a deed of conveyance. The date will be left blank and only inserted when completion actually occurs.

The parties
The names and addresses of all parties to the deed are set out.

Normally there are just two parties, seller and buyer, but occasionally another party is also joined in the conveyance, eg. on a sale of part (*see* Chapter 19) the seller's mortgagee may join in to release the part being sold from the mortgage; on a sub-sale where the seller is conveying direct to the sub-buyer, the intermediate party may join in to give a receipt for part of the purchase money.

Recitals
These are not essential but can be useful in explaining the background to the conveyance, ie. they can explain how the seller came to own the property and the reason for the conveyance. Often they say no more than that the seller is

seised of the estate in fee simple and has contracted to sell it. Such a recital is really superfluous.

Where a recital is useful is in the case of a sale by a surviving beneficial joint tenant. A recital will state that the property was conveyed to the joint tenants, record the death of one of them and state that the survivor is now solely and beneficially interested. Recitals are also useful in sales by PRs (*see* Chapter 18, para. 18.1.3).

The *testatum*

In a traditional deed of conveyance this is the part which says 'now this deed witnesses as follows'. In more modern forms of conveyance, it is often omitted.

The consideration and receipt clause

This serves exactly the same purposes as the consideration and receipt clause in a Land Registry transfer (*see* Chapter 11, para. 11.3.1).

Operative words

These will state that the seller 'hereby conveys' the property and will specify whether they do so 'with full title guarantee' or 'with limited title guarantee' (*see* Chapter 8, para. 8.6.1).

The parcels clause

This is the physical description of the property being conveyed. It may be a freestanding description of the property or it may refer back to what was conveyed in an earlier deed of conveyance.

The description must be complete and accurate. It must accord with the terms of the contract and with what the seller is able to convey.

If there are any rights attached to the land, eg. if it has the benefit of a right of way over neighbouring property, the parcels clause will generally state that the property is sold together with the benefit of rights attached to the property (appurtenant rights). However even if they are not expressly mentioned, the buyer will still obtain the benefit of all rights that go with the land by virtue of s.62, LPA 1925.

If new rights are being created in the buyer's favour, these will need to be expressly stated, eg. new easements being granted to the buyer. This will not arise in the case of a sale of the entirety of the seller's land but only in the case of a sale of part (*see* Chapter 19).

Exceptions and reservations

Exceptions are things that already exist but which are not intended to pass to the buyer, eg. mines and minerals may be excepted from the conveyance.

Reservations are new rights created for the benefit of the seller out of the land conveyed, eg. new easements.

On a sale of the entirety of the seller's land the reservation of new easements will not occur but on a sale of part reservations will be usual (*see* Chapter 19, para. 19.1.4) and they will appear immediately after the parcels clause.

The *habendum*

This describes the estate conveyed, ie. an estate in fee simple, and then specifies existing incumbrances, eg. it may say that the property is hereby conveyed subject to covenants 'contained or referred to' in a specified earlier deed of conveyance. This would mean that the present conveyance is subject not only to the covenants imposed by the earlier deed but also to even earlier ones referred to in that deed.

Co-ownership declaration of trust for sale

Where there is more than one buyer a trust for sale is implied by statute, but the conveyance may expressly state that they will be holding on trust for sale and may then specify their beneficial entitlement. For example, it may say that they are holding on trust for sale for themselves as beneficial joint tenants; or they are holding on trust for sale for themselves as tenants in common in equal shares; or as tenants in common in some other given shares.

This clause frequently goes on to provide that the trustees shall have all the powers of beneficial owners. This is inserted because trustees for sale have limited powers when it comes to mortgaging and granting leases over the property. If the trustees are themselves the beneficiaries this will not be a problem as they can, as beneficial owners, give themselves as trustees full powers to deal with the land, but if they are holding for other beneficiaries their powers as trustees will be limited.

Declarations

On a sale of part there will usually be a declaration limiting or excluding the implied grant rules (*see* Chapter 19, para. 19.1.3).

There may also be a declaration as to who owns which boundaries.

Express covenants

Where the land is sold subject to existing covenants, the buyer normally enters into an indemnity covenant (*see* Chapter 11, para. 11.3.1).

On a sale of part there will usually be new covenants entered into pursuant to the terms of the contract (*see* Chapter 19, para. 19.1.1).

Acknowledgement and undertaking

This applies on a sale of part where title deeds are retained by the seller (*see* Chapter 19, para. 19.3.4).

Certificate of value

This is included if appropriate (*see* Chapter 4, para. 4.2).

Schedules

These are particularly likely to be found on a sale of part where new easements are being granted and reserved and new covenants imposed. Rather than setting out the detail of the new covenants and easements in the body of the conveyance, it is often neater to set them out in schedules.

If one deed of conveyance is being used to convey several parcels of land it may also be convenient to set out the description of the different parcels in separate schedules.

Execution and attestation

The conveyance must be *signed as a deed* by all parties and their signatures witnessed: s.1, Law of Property (Miscellaneous Provisions) Act 1989.

Note

The conveyance need only be executed by the buyers if they are doing something in the deed, ie. if they are entering into covenants, whether new covenants or an indemnity covenant, or if they are making a declaration of trust.

16.3.2 Transfer under rule 72

Where the conveyance will lead to an application for first registration of title, then instead of using a deed of conveyance you can use a document which follows the same structure as a Land Registry transfer. If the sale is of the entirety of the seller's land and the property can be easily and succinctly described and there are not many incumbrances to be set out in the conveyance, then the Land Registry transfer format may be useful. However, for more complex conveyances the normal deed of conveyance format is preferable.

16.3.3 The mortgage deed

The same mortgage documents can be used for registered and unregistered titles as the operative words 'charge by way of legal mortgage' are applicable to both types of title.

16.3.4 Undertaking for discharge of the seller's mortgage

The seller's mortgage will normally be discharged by means of a receipt endorsed on the mortgage deed. A separate deed of discharge, although possible, is in practice rarely encountered where the whole of the security is being encountered. This receipt, known as a statutory receipt, must, unless it is a building society mortgage, name the payer.

If completion is to be on the basis of a solicitor's undertaking the procedure will be virtually the same as that described in Chapter 11, para. 11.3.3 save that the undertaking will refer to the seller's solicitor forwarding the receipted mortgage deed rather than Form 53.

Even though the mortgage may not actually be discharged until after completion, it is important that the receipt should be dated no later than the date of completion.

Statements of account 16.3.5

These will be prepared in exactly the same way as is described in Chapter 11, para. 11.3.4.

Pre-completion searches 16.4

Here there are major differences between registered and unregistered conveyancing.

Central land charges search 16.4.1

The main pre-completion search where the title is unregistered is a land charges search at the Central Land Charges Department at Plymouth.

Registrable incumbrances are registered against the name of the estate owner who created the incumbrance, so the buyer's solicitor will need to search against the names of the seller and all previous known estate owners. The examination of the abstract of title will have identified the names of previous estate owners back to the root document and there may even be references in the root or other abstracted documents to some pre-root names. All known names should be searched against as any charges registered against them will bind the buyer.

There may however be pre-root estate owners who are not mentioned in the abstract of title and consequently the buyer's solicitor will not be able to search against them. Compensation is available to a buyer who is bound by charges entered against these names (*see* Chapter 17, para. 17.3.1).

The central land charges search is not generally made in person but by means of an application for an official search (Form K15).

The advantages of an official search are:

- The result is conclusive in favour of the buyer, ie. if the search certificate states that there is no entry against a particular name and this is incorrect, the buyer will take free from the registered land charge. It will then be the chargee whose interest has not been revealed who must seek compensation from the state indemnity fund.

In this respect the central land charges search differs from both the local land charge search and the district land registry search. These are not conclusive in the searcher's favour and a buyer will be bound by entries that the search certificate fails to reveal, although in such circumstances the buyer will be entitled to compensation. In other words, the enforceability of the entries and the entitlement to compensation are reversed.

- An official search carries with it the benefit of a 15 working day priority period. This means that provided the buyer completes within the priority period of the search they will not be bound by any new entries on the Register subsequent to the date of the search.

Note

As the buyer obtains legal title at completion, it is only necessary to complete within the priority period whereas with a registered title it is necessary to complete and register – hence the longer, 30 working days, priority period.

- The official search certificate protects the buyer's solicitor who will not be liable for any loss arising from error in the certificate.

Making the search

Care must be exercised to ensure that the search is made against the correct version of all names. The definitive version of anyone's name is taken to be the version as it appears in the title deeds. A search in an incorrect version of a person's name will not be conclusive in the buyer's favour. It is similarly important when registering a charge at the Land Charges Department to ensure that the charge is registered against the correct version of the estate owner's name, otherwise the registration will give no protection to the chargee against someone who searches in the correct version of the name.

Note

Registration in an incorrect version of a name will still protect the chargee against someone who does not search at all or who searches in the incorrect version of the estate owner's name: *see Oak Co-operative Building Society v Blackburn* (1968).

In order to narrow down the search, the form enables you

to specify the years of ownership of the names specified and the county in which the land is situated. For example, if you are buying land in Devon which was owned by someone called John Smith between 1960 and 1966 you will, by narrowing down the search, ensure that you do not get a reply which shows every entry against any John Smith who has owned land anywhere in England or Wales since 1925.

The search is actually a search in the index to the various registers that are kept under the Land Charges Act 1972 (previously 1925). The certificate will simply indicate that, say, a C(i) or a D(ii) charge was registered on a certain date but will not give details of the entry. Further details of any entry revealed by the search can be obtained by applying to the Land Charges Department for an office copy of the entry.

The entries revealed by the search should not surprise the buyer. They should all have been disclosed by the seller or known to the buyer at the time of contracting. Any charges registered will bind the buyer and if the buyer did not contract to buy subject to them then the seller is in breach of contract. It will depend on the seriousness of the breach as to whether the buyer is entitled only to damages or is also entitled to refuse to complete.

Sometimes the search will reveal old obsolete entries, eg. C(i) entries in respect of mortgages that have already been discharged or C(iv) entries in respect of contracts that have already been performed. In such cases the buyer should require the seller to try to secure the removal of these obsolete entries.

Relying on previous land charges searches

A buyer will always have to search against the seller's name but may not need to search against the names of all previous estate owners. With the title deeds there may be old search certificates which were obtained by prospective purchasers –buyers, mortgagees, lessees – prior to their acquisition of the property. Provided that the transaction in contemplation of which the previous search was made was completed within the priority period of the search, the then purchaser would have taken free from any subsequent entry and likewise subsequent purchasers will take free from that entry.

Example

- Property conveyed to A.
- A contracts to sell to B.
- B does a land charges search against A which reveals no subsisting entries.
- A's spouse later registers a Class F land charge.

- Completion of the A to B sale takes place within 15 working days of B's search.
- B is therefore not bound by the spouse's Class F charge.
- Years later, B contracts to sell to you and supplies you with the search certificate for their search against A.
- You do not need to do a fresh search against A. You are buying from someone who is not bound by the entry and so you will not be bound by it either.

The same principles will apply to search certificates obtained prior to transactions further back in the title. To rely on an old search certificate you must be certain that:

- The *search was correctly made*, ie. against the correct version of the estate owner's names for the correct period of ownership and specifying the correct county; and
- The transaction in contemplation of which the search was made was *completed within the priority period* of the search.

If these points are not satisfied then you must do a fresh land charges search against the previous estate owner's name and this is very cheap (£1 per name) and quick to do.

16.4.2 Inspection of the property

As with registered titles, you should ensure that shortly before completion an inspection is made of the property to see if there is any third party in occupation. (The rules for determining whether any such third party's interest will bind the buyer are considered in Chapter 15, para. 15.3.1.)

16.4.3 Search of the local land charges register?

The position is the same as that described in Chapter 11, para. 11.4.3.

16.4.4 Company search

Any charges created by a company over its assets must be registered at Companies House otherwise the charge will be void against, *inter alia*, a liquidator of the company: s.399(1), Companies Act 1985. Thus, any fixed or floating charge created by a company over its land requires registration at Companies House.

Prior to 1970, if a company created a fixed charge over land and the charge was registered at Companies House it was unnecessary for it to be registered under the Land Charges Act as well.

Note

Floating charges are *not* registrable under the Land Charges Act.

In the case of an unregistered title it is therefore necessary for the buyer to make a search at Companies House to discover:

- Any pre-1970 fixed charge that might not have been registered under the Land Charges Act;
- Any floating charge whenever created.

The search will also reveal the objects of the company, whether the company has been removed from the register and whether any resolution for winding up the company has been passed.

A company search *must* be made:

- Whenever the present seller is a company; and
- Whenever a company owned the land prior to 1970.

Whether it is necessary to make a search against a company that owned the land between 1970 and the present seller is a moot point. Any *fixed charge* created by such an owner would have required registration under the Land Charges Act if the mortgagee did not obtain the title deeds. Any *floating charge* will no longer affect the land after it has been disposed of by the company as the whole essence of a floating charge is that the charge is only over the property of the company *for the time being* and it leaves the company free to deal with the property prior to the charge crystallising. Nevertheless many people take the view that a company search should be done against *any* company that previously owned the property.

Where the present seller is a company and the company search reveals a floating charge which includes the land in question, the buyer must be certain that the floating charge has not crystallised. To do this the buyer's solicitor needs to obtain a *certificate of non-crystallisation*. This should be obtained from the chargee. Often the buyer's solicitor is offered a certificate or letter of non-crystallisation issued by the company itself. This is *not* sufficient. The certificate/letter should come from the company's chargee.

Note

There is no official search mechanism for making a company search. It has to be done by somebody physically going to Companies House in either London or Cardiff. There are firms that specialise in providing this service and the buyer's solicitor will normally instruct such a firm to make the search. The search should be done as close as possible to completion as it does not carry the benefit of any priority period.

16.4.5 Mortgagee's searches

The solicitor acting for the buyer's mortgagee must ensure that the various searches already discussed are made. Unlike the Land Registry search form (Form 94) which has to specify on whose behalf the search is made, and where it is important to make the search on behalf of the mortgagee rather than the buyer, the application for a land charges search does not specify for whom the search is made. Both the buyer and the buyer's mortgagee can rely on it and obtain the benefit of the priority period.

The mortgagee's solicitor must also search at the Land Charges Department against the names of the prospective mortgagors, ie. the buyers (*see* Chapter 11, para. 11.4.5). Whether this should be a full land charges search or a 'bankruptcy-only' search, as in the case of registered titles, is another moot point. The traditional view was that it should be a full land charges search in the indexes to all five registers that are maintained under the Land Charges Act but as the title will now be registered post-completion a 'bankruptcy-only' search is sufficient.

Self-assessment questions

1 On a sale of whole what are the three main differences between a deed of conveyance and a Land Registry transfer?

2 Will a buyer be bound by land charges which are registered:

(a) against the names of pre-root owners;

(b) after the buyer has made their search?

3 Why does the land charges search only give a 15 working day priority period whereas the Land Registry search gives a priority period of 30 working days?

4 When copies of old land charge search certificates are provided as part of the abstract of title, can the buyer's solicitor rely on them or will they need to make fresh searches against the same names?

Chapter 17

Unregistered freeholds: completion and post-completion

Completion 17.1

There is no fundamental difference between the completion of the sale of an unregistered and a registered freehold title. In both cases the buyer's obligation is to pay the balance of the purchase price and the seller's obligation is to hand over the executed transfer document and other relevant documentation.

Payment will be made in the same way whether title is registered or unregistered.

Verifying the title 17.1.1

The buyer's solicitor will so far have based their investigation of the seller's title on the abstract supplied by the seller's solicitor. Before paying over the price the title must be verified, ie. the abstract must be checked against the original title deeds held by the seller's solicitor to ensure that the abstract is accurate.

Note

This process does not apply to registered titles as the buyer receives office copies of the entries on the Register and then updates that information by the means of a Land Registry search, and the information in those documents is authoritative as to the state of the title.

Where the abstract takes the usual form of an epitome and copy documents the process of verification is somewhat easier than where a *précis* form of abstract has been supplied. In the latter case the originals will have to be very closely read to ensure that nothing important was omitted from the *précis*.

Where there is a long and complex title to be verified it is questionable whether the use of the Law Society's Code for Completion by Post is appropriate. If it is used the seller's solicitor must be given very precise instructions as to exactly what documents are to be verified.

Note

The checking of the abstract against the originals before paying over the price is necessary even where the original title deeds are going to be handed over by the seller's solicitor.

17.1.2 Documents to be handed over

The documentation to be handed over on a sale of an unregistered freehold will be different from that required where the title is registered, as the table below shows.

	Registered	*Unregistered*
1	Land Registry transfer.	Deed of conveyance (or Rule 72 transfer).
2	Land/charge certificate. (There will be as many charge certificates as there are outstanding mortgages.)	All the title deeds including pre-root deeds.
3	If the seller is not identical with the registered proprietor, other documents to link the proprietor with the seller must be handed over, eg. where a surviving co-owner is selling, the death certificate of the other proprietor; where PRs are selling, the grant of representation (*see* Chapter 18, para. 18.1).	These documents will form part of the chain of title.
4	Form 53 for each outstanding mortgage.	The seller's mortgage deed(s) must be receipted.
5	Miscellaneous documents promised by the seller, eg. NHBC guarantees; planning consents. Receipt for chattels if paid for separately.	

Note

With unregistered as with registered titles the evidence of the discharge of any outstanding mortgages may not be available at completion. Completion may take place on the basis of a solicitor's undertaking to forward the funds required to the mortgagee to redeem the mortgage and then forward the evidence of discharge, ie. the receipted mortgage deed, when it is received from the mortgagee.

17.1.3 The passing of the legal title

There is a fundamental difference here between registered and unregistered titles.

Where the title is *registered*, the buyer does not obtain

legal title until the transfer is registered. Although there is no fixed time limit specified for registration, the application should be made within 30 working days of the Form 94 pre-completion search otherwise the buyer will be subject to new entries made between the date of the search and the date of their application for registration.

With *unregistered* titles the legal title passes to the buyer on completion but first registration of title is compulsory whenever there is a conveyance on sale of the freehold: s.123, LRA 1925. The application for first registration must be made within *two months* of completion otherwise the legal title that vested in the buyer at completion will revert to the seller. The seller will then hold the legal title on trust for the buyer.

An application may be made to the Land Registry for late registration. The application must explain the reason for the delay but it will invariably be accepted. If it were not, there would have to be a fresh (confirmatory) conveyance from the seller to the buyer. This the seller could not refuse as the seller is holding the legal title on trust for the buyer. The buyer would not have to pay again for the property but would have to pay the seller's costs.

Post-completion 17.2

Seller's solicitor 17.2.1

If an undertaking has been given for the discharge of an outstanding mortgage, this must be complied with. You will need to send to the mortgagee not only the funds required to discharge the mortgage but also the mortgage deed itself (which will have been obtained with the other title deeds from the mortgagee at the outset of the transaction) so that the mortgagee can endorse on it the statutory receipt.

Buyer's solicitor: stamping 17.2.2

The requirements are exactly the same as for a Land Registry transfer, ie. AV duty at 1% of the consideration unless the conveyance contains a certificate of value and PD stamping to show delivery of the particulars delivered form to the Inland Revenue.

You must submit the deed of conveyance to the Inland Revenue for AV and PD stamping before the application for first registration of title is made. If there is no AV duty payable the particulars delivered form can be lodged at the district land registry at the same time as the application for first registration.

17.2.3 Buyer's solicitor: first registration of title

The application for first registration of a freehold title is made on Form 1B. The solicitor making the application certifies that they have examined the title and are satisfied with it and that all incumbrances are being declared. The Land Registry will then examine the title itself and decide on the basis of that examination whether to grant the applicant absolute, possessory or qualified title.

Documents to be produced

All the documents relating to the seller's title and to this particular transaction leading to the application for first registration must be produced, specifically:

- The *root of title* and *all deeds* comprising links in the chain of title down to the present seller (including the seller's mortgage(s) with receipt(s) endorsed thereon).
- The *contract of sale*, the *property information form* and all *searches and enquiries* made in connection with this transaction, eg. local land charges search, enquiries of the local authority, central land charges searches.
- *Requisitions on title* and the *replies* to them.
- The *deed of conveyance* (or Rule 72 transfer) plus a certified copy.
- The buyer's new *mortgage* (if any) plus a certified copy.

All these documents are listed on Form A13 which is submitted in triplicate together with the original documents, the Form 1B application form and the appropriate fee.

On receipt of the application the Land Registry checks the documents received against the A13 list and returns one copy of the list as evidence of receipt. When the registration is complete and the Land Registry issues the appropriate land/charge certificate, a second copy of the Form A13 will be returned showing which documents are being returned and which have been retained by the Land Registry. The third copy of the list is retained permanently by the Land Registry.

Requisitions on title

In examining the application for first registration the Land Registry may raise requisitions on the title. The buyer's solicitor will have to answer these satisfactorily if the client is to obtain absolute title. It is therefore vital that you have throughout the transaction obtained all the information necessary to answer any Land Registry requisitions which may arise.

Where the seller has given full or limited title guarantee they must assist with any queries that the Land Registry may raise on the buyer's application for registration (*see* Chapter 8, para. 8.6.1). In order to ensure that the seller's solicitor cooperates, it is advisable that if in the course of the transaction you encounter problems which you suspect may lead the Land Registry to raise requisitions, you obtain from the seller's solicitor their personal undertaking to assist in dealing with them.

The pre-registration deeds 17.2.4

It is always difficult to know what should be done with the pre-registration title deeds. Now that the title has been registered they no longer constitute the estate owner's proof of title and are therefore largely superfluous.

There are, however, two particular situations in which the old deeds still have a role to play.

1 *Indemnity covenant.* In the conveyance the buyer may have given the seller an indemnity in respect of existing covenants. When the buyer comes to sell they will therefore need to take an indemnity from the next buyer. However, the fact that the buyer (the first registered proprietor) gave an indemnity will not be indicated on the Register. The solicitor acting on such an occasion will therefore need to look back at the conveyance to the first proprietor, ie. the conveyance leading to first registration, to see if an indemnity was given and therefore whether one should be taken in the subsequent transfer.

Note

If, in the subsequent transfer, the buyer gives an indemnity then, because the transfer is not returned to the buyer, the Land Registry will make a note of the indemnity on the Proprietorship Register. Thus, a note is made where an indemnity is included in a transfer but not where it is included in the conveyance leading to first registration.

2 *General boundaries rule.* The Land Registry operates a general boundaries rule. This means that the filed plan only gives a general indication of the boundaries of the property and does not indicate who has responsibility for the various boundaries. The title deeds may contain more detailed information as to the boundaries and responsibility for them and so it can sometimes be useful to look back at the pre-registration deeds if there is a boundary dispute relating to property.

17.3 Remedies

The remedies for delayed completion, non-completion, breach and misrepresentation are the same as those described in Chapter 13 relating to registered titles.

17.3.1 Post-completion

The position is basically the same as that explained in Chapter 13 *except* that there is a further remedy which may be available to a buyer under s.25, LPA 1969. This may provide compensation where post-completion the buyer discovers that they are bound by a charge registered under the Land Charges Act which their search failed to reveal because they did not search against the name against which the charge was registered.

Section 25 deals with the problem that arises because the seller only has to deduce title back to a good root which is at least 15 years old. Consequently the buyer will not discover the names of pre-root owners (unless they are referred to in the root or subsequent deeds) and therefore no search will be made against those names. However, if there are any charges registered against the names of those estate owners the buyer will still be bound by them. This is obviously very hard on the buyer and s.25 accordingly provides that in such circumstances the buyer will be entitled to seek compensation from state funds.

This compensation is only available if the buyer has investigated title for the normal statutory period. If a root less than 15 years old has been accepted by the buyer, then their failure to discover certain pre-root names will be due to their own acceptance of a short title and not to the operation of the 15-year rule and they will not be entitled to compensation in respect of entries they would have discovered had they not accepted a short title (*see* Chapter 14, para. 14.1.2).

Note

Section 25 does not apply to provide compensation for a lessee who is granted a lease out of an unregistered freehold as it is not the operation of the 15-year rule for roots of title that prevents the lessee discovering the names of certain estate owners to search against but the operation of the open contract rule that a lessee is not entitled to see evidence of the freehold title (*see* Chapter 22, para. 22.1.1).

Self-assessment questions

1 How does an application for first registration differ from an application to register a transfer of an already registered title as regards:

(a) The time limit (if any) for registering;

(b) The purpose of the documents which accompany the application for registration?

2 What are Land Registry requisitions and who must deal with them?

3 If you are selling for a client who is the first registered proprietor, why may you need to look back at the conveyance by which they acquired legal title?

4 In what circumstances will a buyer be entitled to compensation under s.25, LPA 1969?

Chapter 18

Special dispositions

Dispositions by personal representatives 18.1

Legal title will only pass to personal representatives where a sole or last surviving proprietor/estate owner dies.

Proof of the PR's title 18.1.1

To become registered as proprietors of a *registered title*, the PRs will need to produce to the Land Registry a *grant of representation*. However, the PRs will not hold the legal title for long but will either sell the property or assent to its vesting in a beneficiary. This they can do without ever themselves being registered as proprietors.

In the case of an *unregistered title* the abstract will include the death of the estate owner and the grant of representation. A copy of the grant must be supplied to the buyer.

Note

A copy of the death certificate is not necessary as the grant is itself proof of death.

Assents by PRs 18.1.2

Where PRs transfer title to a beneficiary they do so by means of an assent. This must be in writing but need not be by deed and is therefore an *exception* to the normal rule that a legal estate can only be created or transferred by deed.

Registered titles

In the case of a registered title the assent must be in a prescribed Land Registry form.

An assentee applying to the Land Registry to become the new proprietor must lodge:

- The deceased's *land certificate;*
- A certified copy of the *grant of representation;*
- The *assent.*

An assentee can, however, dispose of the title without ever being registered as proprietor. The buyer from an assentee will have to lodge at the Land Registry the above three documents *plus* the transfer to themselves from the assentee.

Unregistered titles

In the case of an unregistered title the buyer from an assentee will similarly need to see both the grant of representation to the PRs and the assent from the PRs to the beneficiary, as they are both essential links in the chain of title.

Memorandum

An assentee is entitled to require the PRs to endorse on the original grant of representation a memorandum recording the granting of the assent: s.36(5), Administration of Estates Act (AEA) 1925. This the assentee should insist on in order to safeguard their position in the event of a subsequent sale by the PRs of the same property.

PR as beneficiary

Where a PR is also a beneficiary then if they are intending to dispose of the property as beneficiary there must be an assent from the PRs to them as beneficiary. Similarly, if PRs are also trustees of any trusts created by the will or intestacy then they will need to assent from themselves as PRs to themselves as trustees: *Re King's Will Trust* (1964).

18.1.3 Sales by personal representatives

All proving PRs must be party to any contract and to the transfer/conveyance although it is not necessary for there to be more than one PR. A sole PR can give a valid receipt for the proceeds of sale and the buyer will take free from the interests of the beneficiaries in the estate: s.27(2), LPA 1925.

There are various other statutory provisions which protect buyers from PRs.

1 The sale will be valid even though it was not necessary for the PRs to realise the property in order to pay the debts of the estate: s.36(8), AEA 1925.

2 Where the PRs have assented to a beneficiary who then sells the buyer does not need to see the will but is entitled to assume that the PRs have assented in favour of the correct person: s.36(7), AEA 1925.

3 'A statement in writing by a personal representative that he has not given or made an assent or conveyance in respect of a legal estate, shall, in favour of purchaser, but without prejudice to any previous disposition, made in favour of another purchaser deriving title mediately or immediately under the personal representative, be sufficient evidence that an assent or conveyance has not been given or made in respect of the legal estate to which the statement relates, unless notice of a previous assent or conveyance affecting that estate has been placed upon or annexed to the probate or administration.': s.36(6), AEA 1925.

Section 36(6) is very important because it enables a purchaser from PRs to obtain the legal title even though the PRs have previously assented the property to a beneficiary. The beneficiary will lose the legal title and the purchaser from the PRs will obtain it.

The operation of s.36

To obtain the protection of s.36 a buyer from PRs must:

- Check the *original grant of representation* to see whether there is endorsed on it a *memorandum* of any earlier assent or conveyance by the PRs.
- Check that the *conveyance* to them by the PRs contains a statement by the PRs that they have not previously assented or conveyed the property to anyone else. (Such a statement will be made in the recitals part of the conveyance and is generally known as a 's.36(6) statement'.)

Provided there is no memorandum on the grant of a previous disposition and provided that the PRs have given the buyer the s.36(6) statement, the buyer will obtain legal title unless there has been a previous disposition in favour of another purchaser, who may be a purchaser directly or indirectly from the PRs.

Example

- PRs assent to X.
- Memorandum of the assent is endorsed on the grant of representation.
- PRs later convey to Y, a purchaser, giving the s.36(6) statement.
- Y will not obtain legal title. The memo on the grant safeguards X's title. If the memo had not been placed on the grant, X would lose the legal title and Y would obtain it.

If there had been an earlier disposition to a purchaser, eg. if X were a purchaser, Y would not obtain legal title even if a memorandum of the earlier purchase had not been endorsed on the grant. It makes no difference whether the earlier purchase was from the PRs directly or from an assentee from the PRs.

- PRs assent to X.
- No memo is placed on the grant.
- X sells to Z.
- PRs later sell and convey to Y giving the s.36(6) statement.
- Y will not obtain legal title because Z is an earlier purchaser obtaining title mediately, ie. indirectly, from the PRs.

The existence of s.36(6) should not be taken to indicate that PRs are in the habit of dealing twice with the same property, but it is something that may occur accidentally. In such a situation s.36(6) seeks to regulate the conflicting claims of the first and second parties.

Section 36(6) would seem to be capable of applying to both registered and unregistered titles. However, where the title is registered, an assentee who fails to get a memorandum of the assent endorsed on the grant but who nevertheless immediately registers the disposition to them and so becomes the registered proprietor, will not be in danger of losing the legal title to a later purchaser from the PRs because the Register is conclusive.

18.1.4 PRs and beneficial joint tenancies

Where co-owners hold for themselves as beneficial joint tenants then the last surviving co-owner will have sole legal and beneficial title. On their death the sole legal and beneficial title will pass to their PRs.

Unregistered titles

A purchaser from the PRs must have regard to the provisions of the Law of Property (Joint Tenants) Act 1964. This Act applies only to *unregistered titles*. (*See* Chapter 14, para. 14.4. Revise that section before reading further.)

Example

- Conveyance to A and B as beneficial joint tenants.
- A dies.
- B therefore has sole legal and beneficial title.
- B dies.
- Grant of representation to B's estate to X and Y.
- X and Y are now selling.

To obtain the protection of the 1964 Act and to be sure of obtaining a good title, the buyer from the PRs will need to:

- Investigate the *title* of A and B back to a good root at least 15 years old;
- Check that the conveyance to A and B is not endorsed with any *memorandum of severance*;
- Do a *bankruptcy search* against the names of A and B to ensure that there was no bankruptcy entry against either of them prior to A's death;
- Obtain a copy of A's *death certificate*;
- Obtain a copy of the *grant of representation* to B's estate;
- Obtain in the *conveyance* from the PRs a statement that B was solely and beneficially interested at the date of death. (Such a statement would normally appear in the recitals.)

Registered titles

In a similar situation where the title is *registered* the buyer will need to:

- Check by means of up-to-date office copies that A and B are the *registered proprietors* and that *no co-ownership restriction* was entered on the Proprietorship Register before A's death;
- Obtain a copy of A's *death certificate;*
- Obtain a copy of the *grant of representation* to B's estate in favour of X and Y.

PRs and tenancies in common 18.1.5

If A and B had held as beneficial tenants in common, then on A's death B would have sole legal title but would hold it on trust for themselves and for A's estate. If a new trustee has not been appointed, then when B dies the legal title will pass to B's personal representatives who will likewise hold the legal estate on trust, partly for B's estate and partly for A's estate.

Generally it is only necessary to have one PR but in this situation a buyer should not buy from a sole PR. (The position is in fact quite complex and goes beyond the scope of this companion.)

Dispositions by attorneys 18.2

A seller (or buyer) may act through an agent. An agent who is to sign a deed on another's behalf must be appointed by deed. The deed of appointment containing the agent's authority/mandate to act is called a *power of attorney*. The person granting the power (the principal) is known as the donor and the person to whom the power is granted (the agent) is the donee/attorney.

General and specific powers 18.2.1

A *general power* entitles the attorney to do anything that the donor could themselves have done. A simple form of general power of attorney is provided for by s.10 of the Powers of Attorney Act 1971 and is set out in the Schedule to the Act.

A *specific power* entitles the attorney to do specific things on the donor's behalf. It will require special drafting.

Trustee's powers 18.2.2

A trustee can delegate trustee functions but not by means of a general power. The power must be specific, for a period not exceeding 12 months and it must be witnessed. A trustee cannot appoint their sole co-trustee (unless a trust corporation) as attorney and any co-trustee must be notified of the appointment: s.25, Trustee Act 1925 and s.9, Powers of Attorney Act (PPA) 1971.

Co-owners hold as trustees for sale and PRs are also trustees. Both are therefore subject to these requirements.

18.2.3 Revocation of authority

The attorney's acts will only bind the donor if:

- The attorney is acting within the *scope of their authority* – this can be checked by examining the power; and
- The authority has *not been revoked.*

Revocation will occur if the donor:

- *Revokes* the power (unless it is an irrevocable security power, *see* 18.2.7);
- *Dies;*
- Becomes *bankrupt;*
- Becomes mentally incapable of looking after their affairs (unless it is an enduring power, *see* 18.2.8).

If the attorney's authority has been revoked then *prima facie* a buyer dealing with the attorney will not obtain title from the seller.

18.2.4 Protection of buyers and other purchasers

Protection available

Section 5(2) of the PAA 1971 provides that if a purchaser has no knowledge of the revocation the transaction shall be as valid as if the power has still been in existence.

Knowledge of an event which causes revocation constitutes knowledge of the revocation, eg. if you know the donor is dead you are conclusively presumed to know that the effect of that is to revoke the donee's authority.

Section 5(4) goes further in protecting later purchasers by providing that in favour of a later purchaser a *lack of knowledge* on the part of the person who dealt with the attorney will be conclusively presumed if:

(a) The transaction between that person and the attorney was completed within 12 months of the power coming into operation; *or*

(b) That person makes a statutory declaration before or within three months after the completion of the purchase (ie. the later purchase) that they did not at the material time know of the revocation of the power.

Section 5(4) is not designed to protect the person dealing directly with the attorney; their protection is s.5(2). However, the Land Registry also applies the conclusive presumption in s.5(4)(a) in favour of such a person. Only where the power is utilised more than 12 months after it was granted does the Land Registry require the person who dealt with the attorney to lodge, with their application for registration, a statutory declaration as to their lack of knowledge of any revocation.

Buyer's actions

A buyer from a seller acting through an attorney must:

- See the *power of attorney* or a certified copy of it to ensure that it covers the transaction in question and, if the seller is a trustee, that the power of attorney is a trustee power;
- Be *unaware of the revocation* of the attorney's authority;
- If the power is being exercised more than 12 months after it was granted (trustee powers cannot be granted for more than 12 months anyway), then a *statutory declaration of lack of knowledge* is lodged at the Land Registry with their application for registration (whether it is an application for first registration or an application to register a dealing) together with a *certified copy of the power of attorney*.

A buyer of an *unregistered title* who, on examination of the abstract, sees that there was at some stage in the past a disposition by an attorney must:

- See the *power of attorney* or a certified copy to ensure that it covers the transaction in question, and that, if the seller was a trustee, the power was a trustee power;
- Check whether the *power was utilised within 12 months* of it being granted; if so the later buyer is protected by s.5(4)(a);
- If the power is utilised more than 12 months after it was granted then check whether there is a *statutory declaration of lack of knowledge* made by the person who dealt with the attorney. This must be made before or within three months of the disposition by that person;
- If the three month time limit has expired the subsequent buyer will still get a good title if the person who dealt with the attorney *did not have knowledge of any revocation* and therefore obtained a good title from the attorney by virtue of s.5(2);
- If that person's knowledge at the relevant time cannot be ascertained, eg. because they are dead, then you must investigate whether at the time the power was utilised the *power was in fact still in existence*, eg. get a statutory declaration from the attorney, or better still from the

donor, that the power was still in existence at the time it was utilised.

18.2.5 Execution of deeds by attorneys

The donor of the power is the seller and is the party to the deed. The attorney merely executes the deed on the donor's behalf.

Section 7 of the PAA 1971 provides that the attorney may either sign in their own name as attorney for the donor, eg. 'Amanda Smith as Attorney for John Ball', or sign in the donor's name, eg. 'John Ball by his attorney Amanda Smith'.

18.2.6 Proof of a power of attorney

Section 3 of the PAA 1971 provides that an instrument creating a power of attorney may be proved by means of a copy certified as a true and complete copy of the original by the donor of the power or by a solicitor or stock broker. Where the power consists of more than one page, each page must be certified as a true and complete copy of the original.

The power may also be proved by means of a certified copy of a certified copy.

18.2.7 Irrevocable security powers

An irrevocable security power is a power granted to a creditor as part of their security for the donor's indebtedness. If it is expressed to be irrevocable it cannot be revoked by the donor so long as the debt exists. For example, an equitable mortgage may give the mortgagee an irrevocable power to enable the mortgagee to sell the mortgagor's legal title and thereby realise the security.

Irrevocable security powers are regulated by s.4, PAA 1971.

18.2.8 Enduring powers of attorney

An enduring power is a special kind of power of attorney which will not be revoked by the donor's subsequent mental incapacity. There are detailed provisions as to the form and effect of such powers under the Enduring Powers of Attorney Act 1985. They are really intended as long-term arrangements and it is not appropriate to use an enduring power when someone is unable to execute a document because of just a temporary absence. (A detailed consideration of them goes beyond the scope of this companion.)

18.3 Dispositions by companies

A corporation in an artificial legal person and its powers

will be prescribed in its constituent documents. In the case of a trading company the powers will be contained in the objects clause of the memorandum of association, although a company registered since the Companies Act 1989 may have an objects clause which merely states that it is a 'general commercial company'. The company should not act *ultra vires*, ie. beyond those powers.

Note

Although the *ultra vires* rule has been abolished in relation to transactions with third parties, it still applies within the company and the members of a company can seek to prevent a proposed *ultra vires* transaction.

If you are acting for a company which is buying land, or lending money to someone else on the security of land, you should check the memorandum of association to ensure that it provides for these activities. On any application to the Land Registry to register the company as the proprietor of the legal title, or of a charge over the land, you will be required to certify that the company has the necessary powers. If the application is made by someone other than a solicitor or licensed conveyancer, the Land Registry will actually want to see a copy of the memorandum of association to ensure that the company has the necessary powers.

However, when *buying* from a company you will have the protection of s.35(1), Companies Act 1985 (as amended by s.108, Companies Act 1989). This provides that the validity of an act done by a company shall not be called into question on the grounds of lack of capacity by reason of anything in the company's memorandum. A third party dealing with the company does not, therefore, have to be concerned as to whether or not a particular transaction falls within the company's powers.

Powers of directors to bind the company 18.3.1

The company acts through agents and the normal rule of the law of agency is that an agent's acts will only bind the principal if the agent acts within the scope of their authority. However, s.35A of the Companies Act 1985 provides that 'In favour of a person dealing with a company in good faith, the power of the board of directors to bind the company, or authorise others to do so, shall be deemed to be free of any limitation under the company's constitution.' Furthermore, s.35B provides that 'a party to a transaction with a company is not bound to enquire as to whether it is permitted by the company's memorandum or as to any limitation in the powers of the board of directors to bind the company or authorise others to do so.'

18.3.2 Execution of deeds

Section 1 of the Law of Property (Miscellaneous Provisions) Act 1989 abolished the need for deeds executed by individuals to be sealed.

Section 36A of the Companies Act 1985 (inserted by s.130, Companies Act 1989) provides that a company need not have a common seal and that a document signed by a director and the secretary of a company, or by two directors of a company, and expressed (in whatever form of words) to be executed by the company has the same effect as if executed under the common seal of the company.

A company that has a common seal can still execute a deed in the old way provided for by s.74, LPA 1925, ie. by affixing the seal in the presence of and attested (witnessed) by its clerk, secretary or other permanent officer or their deputy and a member of the board of directors.

Thus, in favour of a purchaser, a deed will be duly executed by a company if it is executed in accordance with either s.74, LPA 1925 *or* s.36A, Companies Act 1985.

18.4 Voidable dispositions

A voidable disposition is one that can be set aside by certain persons who choose to avoid the disposition.

18.4.1 Dispositions by trustees to themselves

Trustees must not dispose of trust property to themselves unless:

- The trust instrument authorises it; or
- It is sanctioned by the court; or
- All the beneficiaries are of full age and (preferably with the benefit of legal advice) authorise the transaction.

In all other cases the transaction will be *voidable by the beneficiaries*, even though it was at full market value.

There is no time limit on the beneficiaries setting the transaction aside although if they are of full age and know of the transaction and do nothing they will probably be taken to have confirmed it.

These principles apply to personal representatives as they hold the estate on trust for the beneficiaries.

Example

If Peter and Rosa (PRs) transfer property comprised in the

estate to Rosa, the beneficiaries may set the transaction aside. However, if the deceased had contracted to sell the property to Rosa, the PRs in transferring the property to her are merely performing a contractual obligation of the estate and that cannot be set aside. A sale by Peter and Rosa to Rosa's husband or other relative is probably not voidable by the beneficiaries provided it was at full value but the position is not free from doubt and such a transaction is not recommended.

Dispositions affected by undue influence 18.4.2

Where the relationship between buyer and seller is such that one party is in a position of trust/confidence/influence in relation to the other, then a transaction between them may be voidable for undue influence.

There are certain (fiduciary) relationships where undue influence will be presumed to exist unless proved otherwise. They include solicitor–client, doctor–patient, minister of religion–member of congregation, trustee–beneficiary, parent/guardian–child/ward. The husband–wife relationship is *not* one where undue influence will be presumed but is one where undue influence may be proved to have existed on the facts in relation to a particular transaction.

Where the parties are in a relationship where undue influence will be presumed or might be proved to have existed, the vulnerable party must receive separate legal advice.

Note

This is a case where even though the transaction falls within one of the situations mentioned in Rule 6(2) of the Solicitor's Practice Rules, the same solicitor should *definitely not* act for both parties.

Transaction at an undervalue 18.5

There is a danger that such transactions may be set aside if the person making the disposition is later declared bankrupt.

Definition 18.5.1

Section 339 of the Insolvency Act 1986 defines transactions at an undervalue as:

- Gifts;
- Transactions in consideration of marriage;
- Transactions for a consideration which is significantly of lesser value than that provided by the debtor.

18.5.2 Setting aside the transaction

Within two years

The trustee in bankruptcy may apply to the court to have the transaction set aside if it was entered into within two years prior to the presentation of the petition: s.339.

Between two and five years

If it was entered into between two and five years prior to the petition it may still be set aside if the person making the disposition was *insolvent* at the time or *became insolvent in consequence of the transaction:* s.341.

More than five years

If it was entered into *more than five years* previously it may only be set aside if the purpose of the transaction was to put *assets beyond the reach of creditors* or otherwise prejudice such persons – a transaction defrauding creditors under s.423.

18.5.3 Protection of third parties

Section 342 of the Act seeks to protect those who later acquire the property in good faith and for value. As originally drafted s.342 created certain problems which the Insolvency (No 2) Act 1994 sought to address. Unfortunately, this Act itself created further difficulties.

Note

Similar provisions apply in the case of corporate insolvency.

Section 342 (as amended) provides that a later purchaser will be presumed not to have acted in good faith, and therefore will not protected, if:

- They had notice of the relevant surrounding circumstances, ie. that there had been an earlier transaction which amounted to a preference; *and*
- They had notice of the relevant proceedings, ie. that the bankruptcy petition had been presented or that an order had been made.

The fact that there has been a previous disposition by way of gift will, in the case of an unregistered title, be apparent from the abstract of title. Where the title is registered the Register *may* state that a particular transaction was by way of gift and so warn a later purchaser of the possibility that it might be set aside. However, in the case of transactions at an undervalue, other then by way of gift, a later purchaser will probably be totally unaware that the transaction was at an undervalue and therefore will be protected.

Where a later purchaser does have notice that there had

been an earlier transaction at an undervalue (including by way of gift) or one that constituted a preference, it seems that they must now make a bankruptcy search against the name of the donor. Bankruptcy petitions and orders are registered in the Register of Pending Actions and the Register of Writs and Orders maintained under the Land Charges Act 1972 and registration constitutes actual notice: s.198, Law of Property Act 1925. If they do not have a clear search at the time they themselves acquire the property, the later purchaser will not be protected by s.342.

In the case of an unregistered title, this means that you should not rely on an earlier land charges search made against the donor as a previous estate owner but that you should make a fresh bankruptcy only search against that name.

In the case of a registered title opinions differ. Some consider that, assuming the name of the donor can be discovered, a bankruptcy search should be made. Others consider it unlikely that the courts would attach such importance to the registration of land charges when dealing with registered titles but that in the meantime a search is advisable.

Summary
If you are buying property which you know was, within the previous five years, the subject of a transaction at an undervalue or a preference, you will not be protected if you have notice of a bankruptcy petition or order against the donor. You will be fixed with notice if the petition or order is registered under the Land Charges Act 1972 and therefore you should search against the donor's name.

Miscellaneous dispositions 18.6

There are many other people who are in a special position when it comes to buying or, more particularly, selling land. It is beyond the scope of this companion to consider all of them but you should nevertheless be aware that:

- A minor, ie. anyone under 18 years of age, cannot hold a legal estate in land and that any purported transfer to a minor can only give the minor a beneficial interest and not legal title;
- Special steps will need to taken if you are buying from:
  - a charity;
  - a person who is a patient under the Mental Health Act 1983;
  - a tenant for life under a strict settlement.

18.7 Dispositions other than sales

The focus of this companion has been on sales. We have concentrated on ensuring that the buyer, and consequently the buyer's mortgagee, will obtain a good title and on the incumbrances that may burden that title.

The principles and processes involved are, however, equally applicable to a situation where an existing owner is creating a new mortgage. In such a case the owner/mortgagor is in a similar position to a seller and the mortgagee is in a similar position to a buyer. The solicitor acting for the mortgagee will therefore need to carry out the same investigations of title, searches and enquiries as if acting for a buyer.

The various statutory provisions which protect buyers, eg. provisions regarding overreaching, s.5, Powers of Attorney Act 1971; s.36, Administration of Estates Act 1925; s.4, Land Charges Act 1972, protect 'purchasers', a term which includes mortgagees and also lessees. A new lessee is therefore also in the position of a buyer and in acting for a lessee you will consequently do more or less the same as you would do when you are acting for a buyer of a freehold (*see* Chapter 22).

18.8 Auction sales

So far we have assumed that the sale is by private treaty, which means that until contracts are exchanged the buyer's solicitor has an opportunity to negotiate changes to the draft contract and to make various searches and enquiries.

At a sale by public auction the various bids constitute offers and the auctioneer accepts the highest bid by banging the hammer and the parties are then legally bound.

Note

Auction sales are *not* subject to the requirements of s.2, Law of Property (Miscellaneous Provisions) Act 1989 and therefore the contract does not have to be in writing.

Before the auction takes place the draft contract will be available for inspection but prospective bidders will be unable to negotiate changes to it. They must ensure that they carry out and are happy with all their pre-contract searches and enquiries, and with the results of their survey before they participate in the auction.

Self-assessment questions

1 What is a s.36(6) statement? Where is it made and what is its effect?

2 Where an abstract of title includes a disposition by an attorney, why must the present buyer:

(a) See a copy of the power of attorney;

(b) Check when the power was granted?

3 If you are buying from a company, do you need to check that the transfer/conveyance by the company has the company's seal affixed to it?

4 Why may it be dangerous to buy land from someone who received it as a gift?

Chapter 19

Sales of part

Creation of new covenants and easements 19.1

This section applies to both registered and unregistered titles.

On a sale of part of the seller's land new covenants and easements will generally be created. You will need to take instructions from the seller as to what covenants and easements are to be provided for in the draft contract and the buyer must consider whether those proposed by the seller are acceptable and whether any others need to be negotiated.

Both sides need to consider:

- *Access to their property* for themselves, their visitors, animals or vehicles. The route of a right of way, its width and hours of usage need to be defined.
- *Services for their property*, eg. water, gas, electricity, drainage, cable TV. If these are already in place an easement to use them will be required. If not, a right to lay new pipes, cables, etc. will also be necessary.
- Arrangements for the *repair and maintenance of easements*. Who is to pay? Will there be a right to go onto the other's land in an emergency, eg. if there is a blocked drain?
- *Easement of support* where a building adjoins a neighbouring building.
- *Easements of light and air* – if either side acquires these it may hamper the development of the neighbouring (servient) land and therefore have a similar effect to the imposition of restrictive covenants.
- *Are restrictions on the development of the other's property desirable*? Such restrictions may be absolute, eg. residential use only, or qualified, eg. no building without the consent of the owner of the neighbouring land, but even if qualified there is with freehold covenants no proviso that consent cannot be unreasonably withheld (compare leasehold covenants: *see* Chapter 21).
- *Are positive obligations to be imposed*, eg. to build and maintain a fence between the properties? Remember that the burden of such a covenant will not run with the land and therefore it can only be enforced against the original covenantor.

19.1.1 New covenants

These are frequently imposed on the part sold for the benefit of the seller's retained land. If the buyer is in a strong negotiating position, the seller may also enter into covenants for the benefit of the part sold.

Assuming that it is the buyer who is to enter into covenants, a special condition in the contract will provide that 'The buyer shall in the transfer enter into a covenant in the following terms ...'. The condition will then set out the exact wording of the covenant which is to be included in the transfer. To ensure that the burden and the benefit of the covenant will run with the respective estates, ie. with the seller's land and with the buyer's land, the wording will generally state that the covenant is imposed '... for the benefit of the seller's retained land and each and every part of it.' and that it is imposed '... with the intent that it shall bind the land transferred into whoever's hands it may come.'

Note

If existing covenants affecting the seller's land were imposed using a similar form of words, then on a subsequent sale of part, the part sold, as well as the part retained, will be bound by the existing covenants.

19.1.2 Grant of new easements

A special condition will provide for the transfer to include an express grant of easements to the buyer. Even though certain easements might be impliedly granted in the buyer's favour by virtue of the operation of s.62, LPA 1925 or the rule in *Wheeldon v Burrows* (1879), it is not desirable for either party to rely on the implied grant rules because the extent of easements thereby granted might be a matter of dispute. When an easement is expressly granted its scope can be clearly stated, eg. the route of a right of way can be marked on a plan and specific arrangements made for its maintenance.

19.1.3 Preventing new easements being granted by implication

The implied grant rules may result in easements being granted to the buyer that the seller does not intend the buyer to have. They constitute a trap for the unwary seller and the seller's solicitor should ensure that the contract provides for them to be excluded, or at least limited.

Standard Condition 3.3.2 provides that the buyer will have no right of light or air over the retained land but this only limits the implied grant rules to prevent implied easements of light and air arising. If the seller wishes to exclude implied easements entirely, a *special condition* will be necessary to provide that the buyer shall have no rights whatsoever over the retained land other than those expressly granted.

It is not sufficient for the contract alone to limit or exclude the implied grant rules because they will operate on the transfer/conveyance. The contractual provision must therefore be followed up with a *declaration in the transfer/conveyance* that the buyer shall have no right of light or air over the retained land, or no rights whatsoever if a special condition has so provided.

It is also common to include in the declaration a provision that any right exercised in future by the buyer over the retained land shall be deemed to be exercised with the seller's permission. This is designed to prevent the future acquisition of easements by prescription.

Reservation of new easements 19.1.4

Section 62, and the rule in *Wheeldon v Burrows* do not operate in a seller's favour to create implied reservations. However, SC 3.3.2 provides '... the seller and the buyer will each have the rights over the land of the other which they would have had if they were two separate buyers to whom the seller had made simultaneous transfers of the property and the retained land.'

Where a seller sells both parts of the land simultaneously to two different buyers, each will acquire *Wheeldon v Burrows* type easements over the land of the other (the rule in *Schwann v Cotton* and SC 3.3.2 has the effect of entitling the seller to be treated as if they were themselves a buyer of part.

SC 3.3.3 provides that either party may require that the transfer contains appropriate terms, and if the seller wishes to have the benefit of the reservation provided for by SC 3.3.2 the transfer/conveyance must contain an express reservation of such easements as would fall within the rule in *Wheeldon v Burrows*. The precise scope of these is likely to be uncertain and it is therefore always preferable for a special condition to stipulate precisely the easements that the seller is entitled to reserve.

Procedures: registered title 19.2

Where the seller is disposing of part of a registered title the procedure to be followed will differ slightly from that described in earlier chapters which dealt with a sale of the entirety.

19.2.1 Description of the property

Both the contract and the transfer will refer to the title number but make it clear that what is being sold is only a part of the registered title. There must be a clear verbal *description* of the part being sold and also a plan which shows clearly the part being sold and the part retained, and the route of any easements being created over either property.

The plan should be to scale, in which case the contract will usually say that the property is 'more particularly delineated' on the plan. This means that the plan prevails over the verbal description. If the plan is 'for identification only', in the event of a conflict between them the verbal description will prevail over the plan.

Note

Plans in Land Registry transfers must be signed by the transferor and by or on behalf of the transferee and in both registered and unregistered conveyancing it is advisable to follow this practice whenever a plan is used.

19.2.2 Discharge of seller's mortgage

Where the entire property is mortgaged it will be necessary to get the mortgagee to release the part being sold from the mortgage. It will be a matter for negotiation between the seller and their mortgagee as to whether the mortgagee is prepared to release part of their security. Some reduction in the outstanding debt may be required. At completion the buyer will need to receive from the seller a Form 53 (or a satisfactory undertaking from the seller's solicitor for a Form 53) relating to the part sold.

19.2.3 Pre-completion search

The Form 94A Land Registry search is a search in respect of the whole of the land comprised in a particular title. A slightly different form – Form 94B – is used to search in respect of part only of the title. The application must normally be accompanied by a plan in duplicate showing the precise extent of the land to be searched.

19.2.4 Form of the transfer

This will not be a Form 19 transfer, which is a transfer of the whole of a registered title, but a Form 20. This will contain the covenants and easements provided for by the contract and a declaration to limit or exclude the operation of the implied grant rules. It will also contain a plan. (*See* also 19.2.1.)

Placing the seller's land certificate on deposit 19.2.5

The seller will not wish to hand over their land certificate to the buyer at completion but the certificate will need to be produced to the Land Registry for the transfer of part to be registered. Prior to completion the seller will therefore place the land certificate on deposit at the Land Registry and obtain for it a deposit number. This will be advised to the buyer on completion.

Where the property is mortgaged the land certificate will already be at the Land Registry but the mortgagee will have a charge certificate. When the seller arranges with their mortgagee for the release of the part being sold from the mortgage they must also arrange for the mortgagee to place the charge certificate on deposit at the Land Registry.

Registration of the transfer 19.2.6

Following completion the transfer must be registered within the 30-working day priority period of the Form 94B search. When applying for registration the buyer's solicitor will quote the deposit number so that the Registry can locate the certificate.

The buyer will be registered as the first proprietor of the part sold and given a new title number. Easements reserved by the seller and covenants entered into by the buyer will be entered in the Charges Register of the new title and any easements granted for the benefit of the part sold will be noted in the Property Register. A new land certificate will be issued to the buyer. The seller's title will be amended to show the removal from it of the land sold and to record easements and covenants affecting the retained land. The amended land certificate will then be returned to the seller (or amended charge certificate to the seller's mortgagee).

Procedures: unregistered title 19.3

This section considers the differences between the steps to be taken on a sale of part and those described in Chapters 15–17.

Description of the property 19.3.1

In both the contract and the conveyance, the land sold and the land retained should be precisely defined and a plan should always be used (*see* 19.2.1).

Discharge of the seller's mortgage 19.3.2

The mortgagee's release of the part sold is effected either by the mortgagee joining in the conveyance of part to release that part from the mortgage or by a separate deed of discharge (release) for that part.

19.3.3 The deed of conveyance

The deed will contain the easements and covenants provided for by the contract and a declaration to limit or exclude the operation of the implied grant rules.

Although the conveyance of part will be handed to the buyer at completion, the earlier deeds will be retained by the seller as they remain the seller's proof of title to the retained land. They are, however, also proof of the buyer's title and the conveyance will therefore include a list of them and an acknowledgement, and possibly an undertaking, in respect of them.

19.3.4 Acknowledgements and undertakings

Under the open contract rules a buyer is entitled to receive a statutory acknowledgement and undertaking in respect of documents of title which are retained and not handed over to the buyer.

'Statutory acknowledgement and undertaking' means an acknowledgement and undertaking in accordance with s.64, LPA 1925. The *acknowledgement* is an acknowledgement of the buyer's right to inspect the originals and to receive (at the buyer's expense) copies of them. The *undertaking* is an undertaking for their safe custody.

Note

Traditionally, someone who holds the deeds in a fiduciary capacity, eg. a trustee or personal representative, only gives an acknowledgement for production and does not give an undertaking for safe custody.

An acknowledgement and/or undertaking can only be given by someone who is in *possession* of the deeds. If the retained land is mortgaged the title deeds will be in the possession of the mortgagee and the seller cannot therefore give an acknowledgement or undertaking and the open contract rules do not require the seller to obtain an acknowledgement for production from the mortgagee.

The benefit and burden of acknowledgements and undertakings run respectively with the land sold and with the title deeds. If a mortgagee does give an acknowledgement for production it will therefore bind the seller/mortgagor when they redeem the mortgage and recover the title deeds. However, the mortgagee will not have given any undertaking for safe custody (as they hold the deeds as a fiduciary) and therefore the seller will not be bound by any such undertaking unless they themselves give an undertaking when they recover the deeds. This is most unlikely.

The open contract position is modified by SC 4.5.4 which provides that:

> In relation to every document of title which the buyer does not receive on completion the buyer is to have the benefit of (a) a written acknowledgement of his right to its production and (b) a written undertaking for its safe custody (except where it is held by a mortgagee or by someone in a fiduciary capacity).

This means that the seller must arrange for the buyer to have the benefit of an acknowledgement for production from the mortgagee. It does not, however, require the seller to give an undertaking for safe custody when they subsequently discharge the mortgage and recover the title deeds. If the buyer thinks that this is necessary it needs to be provided for by special condition.

Note

The importance of acknowledgements and undertakings is diminishing. Post-completion the buyer of part will have to register title to that part and if absolute title is granted there will be no need for the buyer, at any time in the future, to resort to the original title deeds. They will continue to be important in gifts of part (as they do not necessitate first registration) and those given in the past are still important on current sales.

Marking the abstract and recording sales off 19.3.5

At completion the buyer's solicitor will, as in the sale of the whole, verify the title by checking the original title deeds. As regards those deeds which the seller is retaining, the copies will need to be marked to show that they have been examined against the originals. Each page must be noted to say that it has been examined against the original and to state when, where and by whom this was done. The marked (examined) copies need to be in good order because when the buyer applies for first registration of title this will be the proof which is presented to the Land Registry.

The seller's retained land will remain an unregistered title (unless the seller applies for voluntary registration) until it is itself sold. It is important that the retained title deeds should record the fact that part of the land has been sold off. This is done by means of a *memorandum* endorsed on the holding deed (the deed under which the seller acquired title). The memorandum will generally be quite brief. It will state the date and parties to the sale off and describe the part sold but will not give all the terms of the conveyance, ie. it will not detail all the easements and covenants provided for. It is therefore advisable that the seller should take, and keep with their title deeds, a certified copy of the conveyance of part.

Registration of title 19.3.6

Post-completion the buyer must apply for first registration of title to the part bought within two months. The application will be on Form 1B but the evidence of title lodged will be the marked copies rather than the original title deeds.

Self-assessment questions

1 How can the seller prevent the buyer acquiring implied easements?

2 How can the buyer of part of the seller's land take free from the seller's mortgage?

3 Why must the seller of part of a registered title place the land/charge certificate on deposit at the Land Registry?

4 Why must the buyer of part of an unregistered title ensure that at completion they obtain marked copies of the title deeds?

Chapter 20

Estate conveyancing

Introduction 20.1

It is usual to sell houses on estates freehold but in some parts of the country they are sold leasehold.

Essentially, the sale of a house on an estate is a sale of part of the land belonging to the seller. All the matters which need to be considered where there is a sale of just one part are therefore relevant, eg. necessary *easements*, desirable *covenants*, etc.

The *difference* between selling a house on an estate and a sale of part of the land (*see* Chapter 19) is that, on an estate, the sale will be only one of a number of similar sales of part. It would be neither efficient nor sensible to consider each house individually – the estate as a whole needs to be taken into account. There is therefore a high degree of conformity in the documentation used for each sale. Indeed, there may be a strategy for the estate which needs to be followed for each property, eg. that the front gardens will all be open plan.

The mechanism for selling the properties also needs to be as streamlined as possible to cut down on costs. It is normal, therefore, for the seller's solicitor to prepare and send to the buyer's solicitor at the outset a large package of documents very similar to the documents sent to a buyer under the TransAction Scheme embodied in the National Conveyancing Protocol.

Note

Although estate conveyancing has its own peculiarities and requirements, it is essentially the sale of part of a freehold property and the normal rules and methods for buying and selling will apply. This chapter will highlight the *differences*. If no mention of a particular matter is made, assume there is no difference between estate conveyancing and normal freehold conveyancing on the point.

Seller 20.2

Title 20.2.1

The seller will need to deduce title to the property to the various buyers. If the property is unregistered this will mean finding a good root of title at least 15 years old and deducing all title from that time to the present day.

If the title is registered, office copies of the title will normally be provided. Once the estate layout has been prepared it can be deposited at the Land Registry. This makes the buyer's solicitor's task of undertaking Land Registry searches before completion easier as the description of the plot being bought can be made with reference to the deposited layout plan.

Land Registry Form 102 is also important in estate conveyancing. A file plan of an estate can be large and complicated, particularly if it was originally several pieces of land each with its own rights and burdens. To simplify deducing title in these circumstances, the seller can supply Form 102 instead of a file plan. This form verifies that the plot being sold is contained within the seller's title.

It is far simpler (and usually cheaper) to deduce registered title rather than unregistered. Thus, if title to the estate itself is currently unregistered, the seller's solicitor would do well to consider applying for voluntary registration so that registered title can be deduced to buyers.

Note

Because of the time it takes to obtain first registration, voluntary registration is something that you will need to consider very early in the selling process. Once buyers have been found for properties on the estate, it is likely to be too late.

Whatever type of title is being sold, you need to check it thoroughly. If it contains any flaws these will either need to be remedied or dealt with by way of a *special condition* in the contract barring requisitions.

If the title contains *covenants* which the current development will break, these too need to be dealt with. The alternatives available to solve this problem are covered in Chapter 7, para. 7.6.4.

20.2.2 Contract

The contract will need to contain all the usual clauses for selling either registered or unregistered title, whichever it may be, eg. parties, property, price, deposit, etc. There will, however, be the following additional matters to consider.

Seller's register of title

If the title being sold is registered, the fact that part of the title has been sold will need to be noted on the seller's register of title. To do this the seller's certificate must be deposited at the Land Registry. The Land Registry will provide a 'deposit number' which must be given to the buyer at completion and then quoted by the buyer to the Land Registry when registering the transaction.

The contract will need a special condition providing that the certificate will be deposited and the deposit number given to the seller (*see* Chapter 19, 19.2.5).

Sale before completion of the property

It is very common for plots on estates to be sold before the property is built. In these circumstances, the contract will need to contain detailed clauses concerning the *completion* of the building of the property and the *obligations* on the seller to complete this work to a reasonable standard.

There will be no fixed date for completion if the property is in the course of construction. Instead, the contract will provide for completion to take place within a specified period after the buyer has been served with notice that the property is completed. The normal period of notice is 14 days, but this is negotiable.

Note

It is unreasonable for a seller to become committed to completing a property by a specific date as so much of the building process is liable to the effects of variables such as weather.

Services

The contract will also need to refer to the seller's obligations with regard to services to the property, for example drainage, roadways and landscaping gardens, and state that these will be completed to a satisfactory standard – again with no deadline.

NHBC cover

If the property is to have the benefit of NHBC cover this should be stated in the contract and a contractual obligation imposed that the necessary documentation will be available on completion.

Note

It is unlikely that any house on an estate will be easily marketable without this cover.

Form of transfer

Because of the need for conformity between the houses on an estate, the seller's solicitor would normally draft the conveyance or transfer to be used on the sale of each house, and this would be annexed to the contract. The contract would then provide, by way of special condition, that upon completion the buyer would accept a transfer in the form of the conveyance or Land Registry transfer annexed to the contract. Thus, any negotiation to be carried out in relation to the contents of the conveyance or transfer (the purchase deed) takes place at the pre-contract stage.

Note

Most solicitors acting for sellers of houses on estates are unwilling to accept variations to the standard form of transfer and make this clear when sending out preliminary documentation to the buyer's solicitor.

20.2.3 Transfer

As the sale will be a sale of part transaction, the contract and purchase deed will almost certainly need to contain new *easements* (both granted and reserved) and new *covenants*.

You must give careful consideration to the requirements of each house on the estate, and the estate as a whole, to ensure that each property is granted:

- The easements it requires over neighbouring properties;
- That those neighbouring properties have reserved to them the easements they require over their neighbouring properties; and
- That the character of the estate is preserved by the imposition of certain covenants, eg. leaving the front gardens open plan.

Once the estate is fully sold the seller will not retain any land which is to have the benefit of the covenants given by purchasers of the individual properties and it is therefore common to find the benefit of these covenants being made to run with the land through the mechanism of a building scheme. This enables the owners of each plot on the estate to enforce restrictive covenants imposed on their neighbours.

On the practicalities of drafting a transfer for the sale of a house on an estate, it is normal that the transfer would refer simply to the house or plot number as the property being sold. The detailed rights being granted and reserved and the covenants being imposed would be contained in schedules to the transfer. This is merely the standard method of drafting such documents, commonly used but not obligatory.

What is *essential* is that you consider these points and that they are covered, specifically, in the contract and purchase deed.

20.2.4 Documents provided with the contract

With the contract, you will normally send a large bundle of documents containing other information concerning the property to be sold, analogous to the documentation sent out under the TransAction Scheme, with the aim of putting the buyers in a position to exchange contracts at an early stage.

A property information form will be sent, and possibly also the result of the local search (local land charges search and enquiries of the local authority).

If the property is already constructed and has the benefit of an NHBC documentation, this too will be forwarded.

Roads and drainage

On many estates, almost the last thing to be completed will be the roads. This applies to a lesser extent to the drains. No one buying a house on the estate will want to have their property abutting a private road. While it remains private, they will be liable for its upkeep.

More significantly, if the local authority decides to 'adopt' the road as a public highway, ie. bring it up to their required standards and thereafter maintain it at the public expense, all properties abutting that road will have to contribute towards the cost – which can run into thousands of pounds. The decision on whether or not to adopt a private road is made by the local authority, sometimes against the wishes of the property owners. Thus, it is better to have the estate roads adopted at the outset to avoid this cost later. However, until the roads are completed, no local authority will adopt them.

Note

Liability to contribute is based on the *frontage* of the property abutting the road, not on the size of the plot.

Buyers therefore need to be protected against the possibility that the roads will not be completed, and this is done by a combination of two documents.

1 An *agreement* under s.38, Highways Act 1980 entered into by the local authority and the builder under which the builder agrees that they will construct the roads, pavements, street lighting, etc. to the standards required by the local authority. The local authority, for their part, agree that once this has been done they will adopt the roads and thereafter maintain them at the public expense.

2 A *bond* supporting the agreement between the builder and the local authority. This is to cover the position that might arise if the builder were to become insolvent and therefore become unable to complete their part of the agreement. The parties to such a bond are the builder, the local authority and, normally, a bank. In the bond the bank states

that if circumstances arise whereby the builders are unable to complete the roadways to the required standards, it will provide finance to enable either the local authority or another construction body to complete the works. This finance will have a fixed upper limit.

When both these documents are in place, a buyer can be assured that the road outside their house will eventually become an adopted road, at no expense to them.

Exactly the same principles apply to *drainage to a main sewer* under s.104, Water Industry Act 1991 and agreements and bonds also need to be seen in respect of these.

Note

In order to be able to provide these to a buyer's solicitor, the seller will need to have negotiated and put in place these agreements and bonds at an early date in the preparation for selling the estate, ideally long before buyers are sought.

20.3 Buyer

On receipt of the substantial bundle of documents forwarded by the seller's solicitor, you will need to consider in detail both the contract and transfer.

20.3.1 Contract

The normal contract terms, eg. parties, price, etc. need checking as do any special conditions dealing with faulty title. These are dealt with in the same way as on an ordinary freehold sale. In addition, the detailed terms of the contract dealing specifically with the problems of a house on an estate, need to be considered. For example:

- Are the terms dealing with construction of the property adequate?
- Although no specific deadline for completing the building work will be given, are the sellers at least obliged to construct the property within a reasonable time?
- Are the other terms relating to completion of the estate in general – roads, landscaping, etc. – adequate and reasonable?
- Do they meet your client's requirements/expectations?

20.3.2 Transfer

The *easements* granted and reserved in the transfer and the *covenants* imposed all need to be carefully considered to see that they give the buyer adequate protection and impose nothing too onerous.

Note

As the transfer is to be incorporated in the contract, there will be no opportunity for varying it once contracts have been exchanged, so this is the stage at which you need to negotiate its form and content.

Searches, enquiries and title investigation 20.3.3

The information given on the *property information* form needs to be carefully looked at and all the *supporting documentation* on such matters as NHBC, road and drainage agreements, planning permission and building regulation consents, carefully read.

Note

The mere fact of their existence does not mean that they are adequate for your client's requirements. They all have to be checked to ensure that they do provide the cover needed.

You may also wish to consider submitting *additional enquiries* to the seller's solicitor relating specifically to properties on the estate, eg. when it is anticipated the roads will be finished, perhaps on the likely provision of public transport and/or shops on the estate; the list can become extensive.

If a *local search* has been provided by the seller's solicitor this will need to be checked, eg. how old is it? If no such search has been provided, you will need to carry out one and ensure the result is satisfactory before exchange of contracts.

Other searches may be appropriate and you will need to make these unless they have been provided as part of the pre-exchange package by the seller's solicitor. Examples are *mining* and *commons registration searches*, and a *public index map search* if the title being deduced is unregistered.

Title will normally have been deduced at the pre-contract stage in estate conveyancing. Whatever title has been deduced, it will need to be investigated in the usual way and any requisitions arising out of this investigation made at this stage.

Exchange and after 20.3.4

Once both seller and buyer are satisfied with the form of the contract (incorporating the transfer), and the buyer's solicitor is satisfied with the results of all searches and enquiries, and the buyer has the necessary mortgage offer (if required), exchange can take place. This occurs in precisely the same way as an exchange on a normal freehold sale.

Where the property being purchased is still in the course

of construction, there is likely to be a considerable time between exchange of contracts and completion. In such circumstances, the buyer's solicitor must consider protecting the contract. The contract constitutes an *estate contract* which can be protected by the registration of a C(iv) *land charge* (where seller's title is unregistered) or a *notice* or *caution* against the seller's title (where it is registered).

20.3.5 Completion and post-completion

If the house is finished at the time of exchange of contracts, the contract will have provided for a fixed completion date and completion will take place in the normal way.

If the house is still being built, completion will take place once the buyer has been served with notice that it has been finished. Once this notice has been served, the buyer's solicitor will need to carry out the normal pre-completion searches, obtain any required advance cheque from the mortgagee, and notify the client of the completion date which has now become fixed. Completion will then take place in the same way as a normal freehold purchase.

After completion, the buyer's solicitor will need to take the same steps to protect the buyer's (and the mortgagee's) interest as on the purchase of part of land (*see* Chapter 19, para. 19.2.6).

The only additional point to consider is that if the seller's title is registered, their certificate of title will need to be deposited at the Land Registry so that a note of this sale of part of that land can be made against it. The seller will have deposited their title and received a deposit number from the Land Registry which will need to be quoted in the buyer's application for registration. The contract will have provided for this (*see* above 20.2.2).

Self-assessment questions

1 What is Form 102 and what function does it perform?

2 Make a list of the documents you would expect to send out to a prospective buyer's solicitor with the contract.

3 What post-completion steps are necessary if the land is:

(a) registered;

(b) unregistered?

4 Look at the standard property information form and consider what additional information a client might want if buying on a new estate. Draft appropriate enquiries and then consider how you would view them if you were acting for the builder/seller.

Chapter 21

Leasehold conveyancing

Introduction 21.1

The *similarities* between leasehold and freehold conveyancing exceed the differences: instructions need to be taken, the client kept informed, the TransAction Scheme can still apply, and the same searches and enquiries need to be made before exchange (with the addition of some extra enquiries relating specifically to the leasehold nature of the property). This and the following chapters will emphasise the areas where leasehold and freehold conveyancing *differ*. Where no mention is made of any difference, you can assume that the procedure will be the same as in a freehold transaction.

Note

A solicitor will *not* normally act for both landlord and tenant: *see* the Solicitors' Practice Rules 6(1) and 6(2). Acting for a tenant and their mortgagee is treated in the same way as acting for buyer and mortgagee in a freehold transaction.

Advantages of selling leasehold 21.2

A freeholder may decide to grant a long lease of the property rather than to sell the freehold. To acquire such a lease the tenants will have to pay a large capital sum (premium) and their granting of the lease is therefore a sale of it.

In spite of what has been said above, leasehold conveyancing is more complex than freehold conveyancing. As complexity normally increases cost, there must be good reasons for deciding to sell a long lease rather than the freeholder. The common advantages are as follows.

Rent 21.2.1

A lease will contain an obligation on the tenant to pay rent to the landlord throughout the term of the lease, in addition to the capital sum (premium) which is paid when the lease is granted. In a long residential lease, however, this rent (called the 'ground rent') is usually an insignificant or nominal sum in relation to the other outgoings on the property. Receiving this relatively small sum is not likely to be the deciding factor in considering whether or not to sell a lease.

21.2.2 Continuing interest

The landlord will remain the owner of the superior title, ie. title above the lease being sold. Commonly this is the freehold title, and this companion will treat all leases as if they had been granted by the freeholder, ie. granted 'out of the freehold title'.

You need to be aware, however, that the superior title may be more than just the freehold as a sub-lease/under-lease may be granted out of a head lease, which has itself been granted out of the freehold. The superior title in this case will be both the head lease and the freehold, ie. the superior title will encompass all preceding titles back to and including the freehold. (*See* the diagram below for an example of how this might work in practice.)

When the fixed term of a lease comes to an end the landlord will be able to sell the freehold, free of the lease, or grant another lease out of that freehold. Ownership of this superior title is called ownership of the *reversion*. A landlord therefore has a continuing interest in the property by virtue

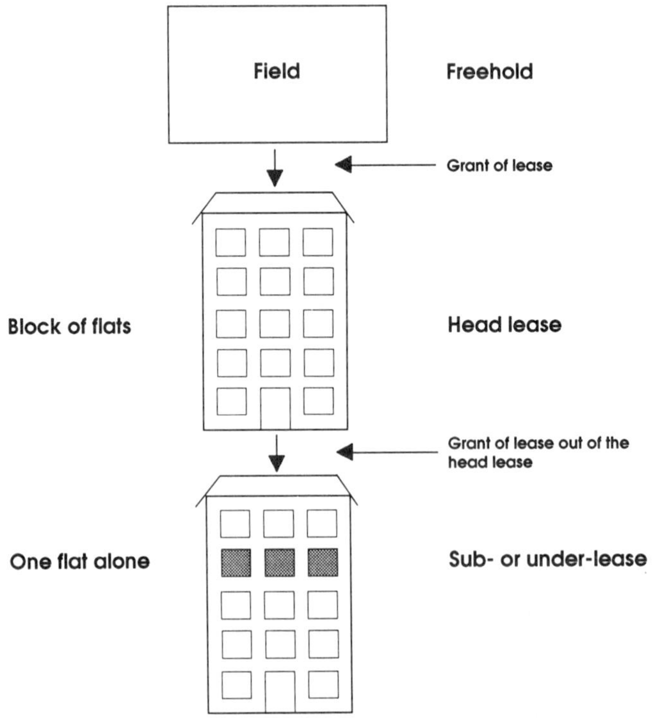

The superior title to the block of flats is the freehold. Superior title to the flat will be the head lease (of the whole block, built on the original field) *and* the freehold. Title to the flat will be the sub- or under-lease of that one flat.

of this ownership. The reversion is worth something, and can itself be sold. Any sale of the freehold reversion will, of course, be subject to the existing lease and the value of the reversion will depend on the terms of the lease, eg. on how long the lease has left to run and therefore when the freehold reversion will fall into possession.

Enforcing covenants 21.2.3

Perhaps the most important reason for granting a lease rather than selling the freehold lies in the area of enforceability of covenants. Where property is sold leasehold, the burden of both positive and restrictive covenants can be made to run with the lease and/or the reversion. For this to be effective, the covenants must *touch and concern the land,* and there must be *privity of estate* between the party in breach and the party seeking to enforce, in other words the parties should be within a *landlord and tenant relationship.*

The burden of *positive* covenants cannot be made to run with the land in freehold conveyancing, except in extremely limited circumstances, so the sale of the property by means of a lease enables a seller who wishes to be able to impose positive covenants against successors in title to the original purchaser to do so easily. This is a great advantage for such sellers. In addition, the sanctions against any tenant breaching a covenant are greater than the penalties incurred by the breach of a freehold covenant (*see* para. 21.4.9).

The grant of a long lease of a house 21.3

When you are instructed to sell a property by means of granting a long lease rather than by selling the freehold you need to consider certain preliminary matters.

Taking instructions 21.3.1

Detailed instructions will be needed from the client on exactly what the lease is to contain.

. How *long* a lease is to be granted? It would be unusual for a residential long lease to be less than 99 years. Such leases are therefore normally granted for this length or longer. The *rent* which is to be paid has to be decided, and whether or not any restriction is to be put upon the *use* of the property, eg. is its use to be strictly limited to residential purposes?

Note

Your client may need guidance on what is and what is not acceptable in a lease if it is to be saleable and part of your job is to give this guidance.

21.3.2 Investigating title

The seller's title will need to be investigated by the seller's solicitor. The title may contain restrictions which would impede the granting of the lease which is being contemplated, and if this is the case the mode of sale will need rethinking or the restriction will need removal (*see* Chapter 7, para. 7.6.4).

Further, any prudent buyer of the lease will want to have the sellers title fully deduced, and it is important for the seller's solicitor to know that this can be done. Any flaws in the seller's title must be dealt with in the contract of sale in the same way as in freehold sales (*see* Chapter 8, para. 8.4).

21.3.3 Mortgagee's consent

If the seller/landlord's title is mortgaged, then it is almost certain that the mortgage deed will require the mortgagee's consent before any lease is granted out of the title over which they hold a mortgage. This is because the granting of a long lease severely diminishes the value of the reversion, which is of course the mortgagee's security.

21.4 Drafting the lease

This is carried out by the landlord's solicitor and submitted to the proposed tenant's solicitor for approval. Only after all its terms have been approved can it be used.

The structure of a lease corresponds closely with that of a conveyance of unregistered freehold land and normally contains the following clauses.

21.4.1 Commencement, date and parties

These will be the same as for a conveyance, save that the wording will be 'a Lease dated ... ' and not 'a Conveyance dated ... '.

21.4.2 Payment of premium and receipt

This is analogous to the consideration and receipt clause in a conveyance.

21.4.3 Operative words

These will read 'hereby leases' instead of the words 'hereby conveys' which you would find in a conveyance.

21.4.4 Parcels

This will be the description of the property, including any easements which it is intended will benefit the property, or which will be reserved by the landlord to benefit adjoining property.

Term 21.4.5

This clause will state the length of the lease and when the lease is to commence. Note that this may be the date the lease is executed, or another date which may be earlier or later. In the case of an estate of houses or a block of flats it will be usual for all the leases to have the same commencement date although actually granted on different dates.

Rent 21.4.6

The rent payable will be stated in this clause, with details of when it should be paid and whether that payment is to be in advance or in arrears. Often payment is fixed on one or more of the usual quarter days. There may also be provision for the rent to be increased in the future, either by a fixed amount or by review procedures which will take into account prevailing market trends. As the tenant will be paying a substantial premium to acquire the lease, normally there will be a fairly small ground rent, not a full market value rent (rack rent).

Express covenants 21.4.7

There are a number of express covenants contained in *most* leases. They are both positive and negative.

To pay rent

The first of these is the covenant to pay rent. This is not the same thing as the last 'rent clause', which just states what should be paid and when. This clause *imposes an obligation* on the tenant to pay. It will be binding even if the landlord is in breach of repairing obligations under the lease and it is not unusual to see the obligation to pay rent continuing even if the premises are damaged or destroyed. To avoid paying rent in the latter circumstance the lease will need to contain a clause suspending rent at such times. It is also common for the rent to be expressed to be payable whether demanded or not.

To repair

A lease will also include a covenant to repair. Either the landlord or the tenant must be responsible for the good repair of the property, and the lease will specify which of them it is.

The *exception* to the rule that this is a matter for the parties to the lease to agree at its outset is the case of a lease of a dwelling originally granted for seven years or less. Here ss.11–14, Landlord and Tenant Act 1985 provide that certain items (structure, exterior, gas water electricity and sanitary installations and space and water heating) cannot be made the tenant's responsibility. The landlord therefore has to maintain and repair these items in property let on such a lease, unless the permission of the court has been granted to opt the lease out of the Act. (Both parties need to apply for such permission before the lease starts.)

Prohibitive covenants

As a general rule, a *qualified prohibition* imposes an obligation on the landlord not to unreasonably withhold consent. This is provided by the Landlord and Tenant Act 1927. Some leases specifically state that the landlord has such an obligation but even those leases which do not so state will have that obligation imposed on the landlord by this statute.

Not to make alterations or improvements This is often present to protect the landlord's ongoing interest in the property. It can be an absolute or qualified prohibition. The former will say, for example 'not to make any alterations or improvements to the property'. The latter will say, for example, 'not to make any alterations or improvements *without the landlord's consent*'. If it is qualified, s.19(2), Landlord and Tenant Act 1927 provides that the landlord's consent cannot be unreasonably withheld.

Note

The landlord cannot ask to be paid for granting consent but can require the tenant to pay any reasonable legal, survey or other costs incurred by the landlord arising out of the process.

Covenant restricting user This covenant enables landlords to protect their security by restricting the use to which a property is put. Such a covenant can again be either an absolute prohibition against a change from a specified use of the property, or a qualified prohibition. Section 19(3), Landlord and Tenant Act 1927 applies to such covenants if they are qualified but there is *no* implied proviso that consent is not to be unreasonably withheld. In other words, the landlord can withhold consent to change of use for any reason whatsoever. (This is an exception to the general rule.) The landlord cannot ask to be paid for granting consent.

Insurance

The property must be insured and the lease must state who is to insure it to avoid the possibility of the property being doubly insured, or left uninsured.

The landlord may want to insure the property and recover the premiums from the tenant. In this case the tenant's interest will need to be recorded on the policy. Alternatively, it may be made the tenant's obligation to insure. The landlord may then stipulate the terms of such insurance, and even require such insurance to be taken out through the landlord's agency.

Notice of dealings to landlord

Because of the landlord's continuing interest in the property which is being let, most leases require that notice of any change of ownership or mortgaging of the leased property is given to the landlord. A lease requiring new tenants/ mortgagees to notify the landlord of these dealings is usually accompanied by the requirement to pay a fee to the landlord for registering such notices in their own records.

Covenant not to assign or underlet 21.4.8

An absolute covenant against assigning or subletting would prevent the lease being sold to anyone else, or another lease being granted out of it, and it would therefore mean that in practice ownership of the property could never pass from the original tenant. Clearly this would be unacceptable in a long lease of residential property and a general bar against assignment or underletting is very unusual in the long lease of a house or flat. A buyer would not accept the grant of a long lease containing such a covenant.

What is more likely is a qualified prohibition against assignment or underletting. This would mean that before a lease can be sold to a new tenant, the landlord's consent must be given. Without such consent any sale would be in breach of this covenant.

Note

It is unusual for landlord to want this level of control over who becomes their residential tenant so that a qualified prohibition against assignment is rare in residential leases.

A prohibition against underletting *part* of the property is very common in order to avoid residential properties being split further.

Where there is such a qualified covenant, the following statutory provisions apply.

Requesting payment for consent

The landlord cannot request payment for giving consent unless the lease provides for it: s.144, Law of Property Act 1925.

Withholding or delaying consent

Consent cannot be unreasonably withheld: s.19(1), Landlord and Tenant Act 1927. Here thought needs to be given as to what might be unreasonable withholding of consent. It is likely to be unreasonable if the grounds given for refusal do not affect the landlord and tenant relationship. The most common reasonable ground for refusal is where a proposed new tenant is unable to provide good references.

If a tenant is refused the right to assign a lease on what they consider to be unreasonable grounds, ie. grounds which do not affect the landlord and tenant relationship, they have a number of options.

- They can *apply to the court* for a declaration that the withholding of consent was unreasonable. If this is granted then the assignment can proceed irrespective of any continued opposition from the landlord.
- They may be entitled to *damages* under Landlord and Tenant Act 1988, which places a statutory duty on a landlord to provide either consent to assignment or reasons for refusal of consent to a tenant within a reasonable time of consent being requested. Breach of this duty may cause the tenant loss, eg. the tenant loses the person interested in taking an assignment, and this loss makes the landlord liable to the tenant for damages.

Quiet enjoyment

This ensures the tenant has full use of the leased property without interference from the landlord (except as maybe provided for in the lease, for example access for repairs).

21.4.9 Forfeiture (or re-entry)

This is a very effective weapon against tenants who breach covenants. When a lease is forfeited it ceases to exist.

Note

No such clause is implied by law. Thus, for a landlord to have the right to forfeit, the right must be expressly reserved in the lease.

Business leases often contain a clause whereby the lease is forfeited if the tenant becomes insolvent (known somewhat inaccurately as a 'forfeiture for bankruptcy' clause). Any such clause in a *residential lease* is *absolutely unacceptable* – because of its effect on mortgageability, a vital requirement for residential property. A lender takes a mortgage over the leasehold title as security; if that title disappears because the lease ends due to forfeiture, their security also disappears. If it disappears due to the insolvency of the tenant, then the cause of their loss of security is the very situation they tried to protect themselves against by taking security (in the form of a mortgage) in the first place.

A forfeiture for bankruptcy clause in a residential lease would therefore make the property almost unmarketable as most buyers need a mortgage to fund their purchase. If it could be sold it would be for a very low price.

Forfeiture can also be a landlord's remedy for breach of other tenant's covenants, eg. paying rent or repairing.

It is possible for the court to grant a tenant relief against forfeiture, but details of how and when this may apply are beyond the scope of this companion.

Certificate of value 21.4.10

Ad valorem stamp duty is payable on the premium paid for the grant of a new lease in the same way as it is payable on the consideration shown in a conveyance or transfer of freehold land. This can only be avoided if the premium does not exceed the stamp duty limit (currently £60,000) *and* the rent does not exceed £600 *per annum*. The lease can then contain a certificate of value as follows:

It is hereby certified that the transaction hereby effected does not form part of a larger transaction or of a series of transactions in respect of which the amount or value or the aggregate amount or value of the consideration other than rent exceeds £60,000.

Stamp duty is also payable on the rent, whatever the premium paid. This is based on the length of the term and the amount of the rent and is calculated with the use of tables provided by the Inland Revenue. Stamp duty on the rent element of a lease is *only* paid upon the grant of the lease. When a lease is subsequently assigned stamp duty is simply paid on the price paid for the assignment.

Production to the Inland Revenue 21.4.11

Leases for seven years or more need to be produced to the Inland Revenue with a completed PD Form.

Note

This companion does not cover in detail several other areas of law which have an impact on leasehold conveyancing in practice. They are not part of the PLC and are not therefore covered in the main text. We strongly recommend, however, that you read them so that you make yourself aware of the potential pitfalls which exist. *See* the Appendix.

Self-assessment questions

1 Once a lease has been granted, what, if anything, does a landlord have left to sell?

2 State two circumstances which would lead you to advise a client to grant a lease rather than the freehold of their property.

3 By what means, if any, can a landlord prevent a tenant changing:

(a) the external appearance;

(b) the internal layout;

(c) the use of the property?

4 What clauses you would find unacceptable in a lease of residential property?

Chapter 22

Grant of a long lease

The draft contract 22.1

Note

This chapter deals with the grant of leases out of both registered and unregistered titles.

The contract is drafted by the landlord's solicitor and will often incorporate the Standard Conditions of Sale discussed in Chapter 8. Also incorporated into the contract will be the draft lease (as agreed between the parties) and a condition of the contract will state that upon completion a lease in the form annexed to the contract will be granted to the buyer.

The contract will be completed as follows:

- *Agreement date:* inserted on exchange;
- *Seller and buyer;*
- *Property:* a description of the property being sold, eg. 15 Acacia Avenue, ... , *and* details of the lease, eg. 'upon completion the buyer will be granted by the seller a lease for x years at a yearly rent of £y the lease to take the form of the draft lease annexed to this contract';
- *Root of title/title number:* will relate to the seller's title;
- *Incumbrances:* this will state any incumbrances on the seller's freehold title (as if that title was being sold). In the same way that the seller of a freehold must disclose incumbrances affecting the title when a freehold is sold, the seller when granting a lease must disclose in the contract any such incumbrances affecting the freehold. To deal with new matters to be created by the lease, the land is also sold 'together with those contained in the draft lease annexed'.

The other clauses in the contract will be completed in the same way as if the property was to be sold with freehold title.

Deducing title 22.1.1

A prudent buyer/tenant will want to see that the seller/landlord has good title to the freehold out of which the lease is to be granted. What has to be deduced to a buyer/tenant depends upon whether the landlord's title is registered or unregistered and whether the open contract rules or the

Standard Conditions of Sale are being applied.

If a lease is to be granted for more than 21 years, the leasehold title will need to be registered following completion of the purchase and, in order to obtain absolute leasehold title, the tenant will need to satisfy the Registrar on all superior titles. The tenant must therefore be able to prove the landlord's superior title in exactly the same detail as if *that* title itself were being registered.

Types of registered leasehold title
As *absolute leasehold title* is the only readily saleable form of leasehold title. Therefore a purchaser will want to ensure that the contract provides for sufficient title to be deduced by the landlord to enable the property to be registered with title absolute.

If the Registrar cannot be satisfied on all superior titles then only *good leasehold title* can be granted to the buyer/ tenant. Although such a title is not totally unmortgageable, it is not very acceptable as security and it is therefore more difficult to find a lender prepared to take a charge over it. This severely affects the marketability of the property.

There are two specific problems with good leasehold title:

- There is no guarantee that the lease has been validly granted;
- The leasehold title will be subject to all incumbrances contained in the superior title although the tenant will not know about them if the superior title has not been deduced in full.

Where the superior title is unregistered
The open contract rule Under an open contract the landlord is not obliged to deduce title to the freehold at all: s.44(2), Law of Property Act 1925.

Because of the need for registration following completion, no sensible buyer, or their solicitor, would accept this, especially if they are paying a substantial premium to buy the lease. The contract must therefore contain a clause requiring the seller to deduce *all* superior titles.

Standard Condition 8.2.4 This provides that where a new lease of over 21 years is being granted, ie. one requiring registration following completion, title must be deduced to a buyer to enable them to register their new title with absolute leasehold title. Even if the Standard Conditions of Sale are not being used, such a clause should be incorporated in any contract where a lease of more than 21 years is being granted, in order to protect the buyer's position, and ensure the future saleability of the lease.

Where the superior title is registered

The open contract rule Section 110, Land Registration Act 1925 does not apply to the granting of a lease and a buyer therefore has no right to see copies of the landlord's title. However, as the Register of Titles is open to public inspection, there is nothing to prevent a buyer/tenant obtaining office copies of the seller's title for themselves.

Standard Condition 8.2.4 (see above) This applies equally to the grant of a lease out of registered title.

Where a lease for more than 21 years is being granted out of a registered title, it will be registered with its own title number. Nevertheless, a note will still need to be made of the grant of the lease against the landlord's freehold title and, in order for this to be done, the landlord will need to deposit their land certificate with the Land Registry.

It must be a condition of the contract that the landlord will do this, and supply the deposit number – which will be given to the landlord by the Land Registry once the certificate is deposited – to the buyer so that this number can be incorporated in the buyer's application to register the lease.

Consideration of the draft contract 22.1.2

The buyer/tenant's solicitor will need to ensure that the lease to be granted, and registered following completion, will provide a good and marketable title, both for the buyer and their mortgagee, if any. The same attention must be paid to matters such as deposit, rate of interest, time for completion, etc. in a sale of a lease as would be given to these matters in a freehold sale contract.

Because this sale is more complex, special attention will therefore need to be paid to other items such as the title to be deduced. If for any reason, SC 8.2.4 has been excluded from the contract, or if the contract is governed by the open contract rules, this will be because the landlord either *cannot*, or *will not*, deduce sufficient title to the buyer to enable them to register with absolute leasehold title following completion.

Because of the shortcomings of good leasehold title, the buyer's solicitor should make every effort to ensure that the contract contains an obligation on the landlord to deduce all superior title, ie. a clause such as SC 8.2.4.

Note

If this cannot be achieved, then both the buyer and their mortgagee (if any) must be informed that only good leasehold title will be granted on completion, and/or the consequences to them of this. Your advice is likely to be that the sale should not proceed, but the decision will be theirs.

As the draft lease will form part of the contract, its wording cannot be changed once contracts are exchanged without the written agreement of the parties. Obviously its terms and conditions will need to be considered carefully *before* exchange (*see* Chapter 21).

22.1.3 Insurance arrangements

As discussed in Chapter 21, the lease will make provision for the property to be insured. Anyone lending money on the security of this new lease will also want to see that the insurance arrangements are adequate, and some mortgagees require that insurance be effected through their own agency. This may be in direct conflict with the proposed terms of the lease if it provides for the landlord to insure and some negotiating will need to be done to ensure that these conflicting interests are resolved before contracts can be exchanged, ie. either the landlord or the mortgagee must give way. Both landlord and mortgagee insuring should be avoided due to the risks of double insurance.

22.1.4 Mortgagee's consent

Where the landlord's title is mortgaged, the mortgagee's consent will almost certainly be needed before a lease can be granted (*see* Chapter 21, para. 21.3.3).

The contract will therefore need to contain a special condition requiring the seller/landlord to obtain this consent and, on completion, to provide evidence that this has been done.

22.2 Exchanging contracts and investigating title

22.2.1 Preparing for exchange: the buyer

The same points arise here as apply in a freehold purchase (*see* Chapter 10).

- The draft contract (incorporating the draft lease) must be approved;
- All usual pre-contract searches and enquiries must have been returned, and their results satisfactory;
- If the seller/landlord's title has been deduced at this stage, then a full investigation of it must have been made to your satisfaction;
- Your client must have their finance arranged in full to enable them to complete the transaction on the proposed date.

Buyer and seller 22.2.2

Both parties need to sign the contract before exchange and you must inform your client of its significance and terms (*see* Chapter 10, the points detailed there apply equally here).

Methods of exchange are exactly the same as for a sale of freehold property (*see* Chapter 10, para. 10.2).

Investigating title 22.2.3

This may be done before or after exchange, as in freehold conveyancing. It is even more common, however, in sales of leases for title to be deduced and investigated *before* exchange.

Just as the seller/landlord's solicitor will need to deduce title to the freehold as if the freehold itself were being sold, the buyer/tenant's solicitor will need to investigate that title accordingly. The same rules will therefore apply to investigating title in this situation as apply when purchasing the freehold (*see* Chapter 14).

This assumes that SC 8.2.4 (or similar) is applied and that the landlord is deducing title sufficient to enable the buyer to register with absolute leasehold title following completion. If any lesser title is being deduced, then the buyer's solicitor will have to apply the same rules for investigating title to whatever documentary evidence the landlord has provided.

Preparing for completion 22.3

Engrossing the lease 22.3.1

A perfect version of the agreed form of the lease is prepared in duplicate. (This is known as engrossing the lease.) It will take exactly the same form as the draft which was previously agreed and annexed to the contract.

It will normally be prepared by the seller's solicitor, which is the opposite of the situation in freehold, where the buyer's solicitor prepares the transfer/conveyance.

If the Standard Conditions are being used, SC 8.2.6 deals with the time limit for engrossing and delivery of the lease to the buyer – at least five working days before the completion date.

Two copies of the lease are prepared. They are called lease and counterpart.

Execution 22.3.2

Both lease and counterpart have to be executed as *deeds*. The lease is executed by the landlord/seller and the counterpart by the tenant/buyer. The same rules apply to their execution as apply to the execution of a transfer or conveyance of a freehold title.

Following their execution both lease and counterpart can be delivered to the other party in escrow, in the same way as deeds can be delivered in escrow in freehold conveyancing.

Note

In practice it is rare for the lease but more common for the counterpart to be delivered in this way.

22.3.3 Pre-completion searches

The buyer/tenant's solicitor will need to carry out pre-completion searches.

Whether the title being deduced is registered or unregistered, pre-completion inspection of the property is always advisable for the same reasons one would carry out an inspection in freehold conveyancing.

Unregistered titles
Where the title is unregistered the buyer's solicitor will need to carry out land charges searches against the estate owners of the superior title. Land charges searches must therefore be carried out against the landlord and previous estate owners of the freehold, for the period of their ownership applying the usual search principles for unregistered titles (unless satisfactory searches against their names have already been provided). (*See* Chapter 16, para. 16.4.)

Registered titles
If the lease is being granted out of a registered title then the usual Land Registry search on Form 94A (or 94B of part) must be carried out against the superior title. This is done on behalf of the buyer if no new mortgage is involved, or on behalf of their prospective mortgagee where the purchase of the lease will be with the aid of mortgage finance.

There is no difference between the situation here and that in freehold conveyancing as regards the searches and method of searching.

22.4 Completion

22.4.1 Documents

The lease and counterpart are *exchanged* so that each party has an identical copy of the lease, executed by the other. The tenant holds the original lease and the landlord holds the counterpart.

If the freehold title is *unregistered*, the buyer/tenant's solicitor will need to see all the original documents of title and mark the abstract or epitome as having been so examined in the same way and for the same reasons as apply to a sale of part (*see* Chapter 19, para. 19.3.5).

If the freehold title is *registered* the tenant should receive the deposit number of the landlord's certificate of title at the Land Registry. If this is not available at completion, an undertaking for it to be forwarded as soon as the deposit number is received by the landlord's solicitor from the Land Registry must be given in its place.

Note

The contract will need to have provided for the abstract of the freehold title or deposit number to be given.

The landlord must obtain the consent of the landlord's mortgagee if the landlord's title is mortgaged and the mortgage deed requires such consent. A request by letter to the mortgagee is the normal method of obtaining such consent. This consent must be handed to the tenant on completion.

Purchase monies 23.4.2

The landlord will receive the balance of the purchase money (premium), together with any apportioned ground rent if the ground rent is to be paid in advance.

Example

Consider a lease which requires ground rent of £100 *per annum* to be paid in advance on the usual quarter days; this will mean £25 being paid on each quarter day. Completion of the grant of the lease takes place on 30 June. Rent has to be paid for the period from 30 June to the next quarter day (29 September) which is 60 days. The rent per day is 100 ÷ 365 = 274 × 60 = £16.44. This sum is the apportioned ground rent payable on completion. (Other sums paid or payable in advance are apportioned by the same method.)

Post-completion stages 22.5

Stamping 22.5.1

The lease itself will need to be stamped with *ad valorem* duty on the premium and on the rent (*see* Chapter 4). The counterpart lease needs to be stamped with a fixed duty of 50p and the landlord's solicitor will need to ensure that this is done. Leases for seven years or more also require PD stamping to show that a particulars delivered form has been completed and delivered to the Inland Revenue.

22.5.2 Registration

If the term of the lease exceeds 21 years it will need to be registered under its own title number.

First registration

If the landlord's title is *unregistered*, the registration of this lease will constitute a first registration and will therefore need to be applied for within two months of completion. If this is not done, the legal title which passed to the tenant when the lease was granted on completion will revert to the seller/landlord. This is the same principle as in freehold conveyancing.

Application to register will be made on Land Registry Form 2B and the following documents will need to be sent to the Land Registry:

- The original lease, duly stamped;
- A certified copy of the lease;
- Evidence of the freehold title – this will be a marked abstract of the freehold title;
- If the property has been mortgaged, the original mortgage duly executed and a certified copy of it;
- The fee.

Dispositionary lease

If the landlord's title is *registered* then this is not a first registration. It is a *disposition* of registered land and until the lease is registered the tenant will not have legal title.

The application for registration must be submitted within the priority period of the Land Registry search taken out against the landlord's title before completion, ie. within 30 working days of the search date, otherwise the tenant will be bound by any new entries that might be made against the freehold title. The application will be on Form 3B and must be accompanied by all the documents listed above save that evidence of title will take the form of the landlord's title number and the deposit number of the certificate of that title.

The grant of the lease will also need to be noted against the landlord's freehold title. This is done by the Land Registry when the application to register the lease is made. It can, however, only be done if they receive the deposit number of the landlord's certificate of title. The note on the landlord's title provides notice to any purchaser of that title that a lease has been granted out of it and they will therefore take subject to it.

Note

1 The nature and content of what appears on the landlord's title to reflect the sale of the new lease will be analogous to the entries made to reflect a sale of part (see Chapter 19, para. 19.2.6).

2 A purchaser of the freehold title *may* be bound by the tenant's interest even if such a notice has not been entered. This is because the tenant will have an overriding interest under s.70(1)(g), Land Registration Act 1925 if s/he is *in occupation* at the time of the freehold sale or in receipt of rents or profits.

Notice to landlord 22.5.3

If the lease contains a clause requiring notice to be given to the landlord whenever the lease is mortgaged, notice of any new mortgage must be served on the landlord and any fee required under the lease paid.

The normal procedure is for a notice in duplicate to be prepared by the tenant's solicitor and sent to the landlord or their solicitor (as the lease requires) in duplicate with a request that one copy of the notice be receipted and returned. This receipted duplicate is then kept with the deeds as evidence that this covenant in the lease has been complied with and the other copy is retained by the landlord as a record.

Custody of the deeds and documents 22.5.4

Once registration of the lease has been completed and the land or charge certificate and the original lease have been returned to the tenant's solicitor, all the deeds and documents (the land or charge certificate, lease and all other documents which will be needed in any sale, for example NHBC documentation, damp proof guarantees and the like) will need to be stored somewhere for safe keeping. If there is a mortgage they must be sent to the mortgagee.

If the property is not mortgaged, the client's instructions must be sought as to where they want them stored.

Self-assessment questions

1 What is the difference between residue and reversion?

2 What title does a seller have to deduce when granting a new lease using the standard conditions of sale?

3 What pre-completion searches are needed if the title from which the lease is granted is:

(a) unregistered;

(b) registered?

4 What post-completion steps are needed and what are the time limits for these? Is your answer the same whether the superior title is registered or unregistered? If not, in what respects does it differ?

Chapter 23

Special problems relating to flats

Introduction 23.1

A flat is normally one of a number of flats in a block or house. In such a situation each individual flat in the block will be the subject of a lease to a particular tenant but there will be parts of the block which are not included in any of the leases, eg. the staircase, the roof, the foundations, the garden, etc. Any part not let to a tenant as their flat will be included in what are called the 'common parts'. The responsibility for maintenance of these parts will not be vested in any individual tenant but will be the responsibility of the landlord. The cost of fulfilling this obligation is not, however, paid by the landlord. Instead, any maintenance expenditure will be reimbursed to the landlord by the tenants via the service charge.

In a block of flats you would expect to find that each lease contains identical terms except for the description of the flat itself and the parties to the lease. A flat lease will take the general form shown in Chapter 21. The matters which require additional attention in a flat lease are:

- Parcels;
- Easements;
- Tenant's covenants;
- Enforceability of covenants;
- Landlord's covenants;
- Management company;
- Insurance;
- Statutory provisions for service charge levying.

Parcels 23.2

Because of the need to know what has been leased to the tenant – and is therefore the tenant's responsibility – and what has been included in the common parts – and is therefore the landlord's responsibility – this clause needs to be particularly detailed and accurate. It will have a direct bearing on the extent of the repairing obligations of both the landlord and the tenant. It is also advisable to have a good plan incorporated in the lease, to assist in this accurate identification.

23.3 Easements

Careful thought needs to be given to the rights the flat owner will need for such things as access to and from the flat and the passage of services over neighbouring flats and the common parts. Also, your client may need the right to enter other flats in an emergency, eg. an overflowing washing machine, or in order to fulfil repairing obligations. These rights need to be specifically granted. It is almost certain that other flats in the block will need reciprocal rights over the flat being sold and these need to be specifically reserved. The landlord will need to reserve a right of access to carry out repairs either to the flat or to the structure of the block.

The new rights are usually subject to giving reasonable notice to the flat owner. In cases of emergency, the need to give notice is waived.

In addition to these rights, each flat will need to grant, and have reserved for it, rights of support and protection to and from all the other parts of the block.

23.4 Tenant's covenants

Flat leases always contain far more covenants than those imposed upon freehold owners. Some of these covenants will be *restrictive*, eg. against nuisance, display of advertisements, the keeping of pets, the carrying out of alterations, etc., but the tenant will also be bound by a number of *positive* covenants, eg. to repair and maintain the flat, to pay rent and service charges.

23.4.1 Enforceability of covenants

Each lease of a flat in a block will contain the same covenants but there is no privity of estate between the individual tenants. This can cause problems. A typical example would be where a lease contains an obligation not to keep pets but one of the flat owners is keeping a dog which is proving to be a nuisance to the others. Each flat owner knows that this constitutes a breach of the lease because all leases in the block contain the same prohibition but, without privity, they cannot take direct action against the neighbour with the troublesome dog.

There are two solutions to this problem, and any lease must contain one or the other or it will be unmortgageable. A lease must contain a clause allowing 'mutual enforceability of covenants' so that tenants have some way of forcing neighbouring tenants to abide by the covenants in their leases.

Enforcement by the landlord

The first method is for each lease of a flat in the block to contain a clause requiring the landlord to enforce the covenants against recalcitrant tenants at the request of another tenant. This can be achieved because the landlord has privity of estate with each tenant and if the landlord were to refuse to take action when requested to do so, the landlord would be in breach of covenant to the tenant requesting action.

Such a clause is normally accompanied by a requirement for the requesting tenant to *indemnify* the landlord against any costs incurred by the landlord in such enforcement.

Letting scheme

The second method is to create a letting scheme (similar to a building scheme in freehold land) which enables covenants to be enforced between tenants without recourse to the landlord. This is less commonly found.

Landlord's covenants 23.5

The most important landlord's covenant will be to deal with the maintenance and repair of the common parts and structure.

If the landlord has decided when setting up the scheme of leases in the block to provide any services, this covenant also needs to make it clear that the *landlord* is to provide services Examples of services might be, garden maintenance and cleaning and lighting of the common parts.

The landlord will also covenant for *quiet enjoyment* in the usual way.

If the method of dealing with the enforceability of covenants outlined in 23.4.1 above is adopted, the landlord will also covenant to require each tenant to observe the covenants contained in the lease of their property.

The landlord can include in the leases a right to employ managing agents to carry out the landlord's obligations, particularly with regard to repair, maintenance and services. The cost of employing agents in this way will form part of the service charge payable by the tenants.

Management company 23.6

A landlord will often not wish to retain any obligations concerning the block once the flats are all sold. They may be unwilling to be responsible for the common parts or any services to tenants. In this situation landlords often divest themselves of these responsibilities through a management company.

Under this system one of two things can happen:

- Three-party leases;
- The freehold is vested in the management company.

23.6.1 Three-party leases

The leases are drawn up in such a way that there are three parties to each of them: the landlord, the management company and the tenant. All the covenants which would normally impose obligations upon the landlord are instead entered into by the management company, and usually the only duty remaining on the landlord is that of receiving rent!

In such a lease, the management company will be responsible for repairs and maintenance, and any services required by the lease. Tenants who have problems with these or any other covenants normally entered into by a landlord would instead deal with the management company on these issues.

The tenants are often made the shareholders in the management company and thereby have a direct say in the maintenance of the block.

23.6.2 Freehold vested in the management company

In this situation the tenants are again the shareholders in the management company but the freehold of the block is vested in that company, not in the landlord, the landlord bowing out of the picture altogether. The result for the tenants is essentially the same, they have a direct say in the running of their block.

Note

Whether a three party lease is involved or the freehold is vested in the management company, where the tenants are shareholders in a management company their share in the management company must be transferred to the new owner when a tenant sells their flat. This will be important where the management company is *limited by shares*.

If, however, the company is *limited by guarantee* then there will be no share to be transferred. For this reason, management companies limited by guarantee are more popular.

23.7 Insurance

The usual problem of who should take out insurance on a leasehold property also arises in connection with blocks of flats. It is almost invariably the case that the entire building is covered by a 'block' policy, on which each tenant's interest is noted. Tenants cannot normally opt out of such a policy.

Any mortgagee of an individual flat will need to ensure that the insurance is adequate. They may be happy with the 'block' policy or may prefer to have their own separate insurance. The dangers of double insurance will need to be pointed out to those who choose the latter course and it is their solicitor's duty to do this.

Statutory provisions for service charges 23.8

It is a common complaint among flat owners that they do not get a fair deal where services charges are concerned. This problem is particularly acute when major works are undertaken to a block, eg. painting the outside, general refurbishment, roof repairs, and the costs thereby imposed on the tenants are high. Tenants often feel they have too little control in these matters.

In an attempt to improve the situation, ss.18–30, Landlord and Tenant Act 1985 made special provisions to protect tenants.

Payment required in advance 23.8.1

It is not unusual for a landlord to set up a 'sinking fund' by which each tenant contributes some money each year (through their service charge payments) towards a fund which is not immediately expended on current maintenance. This fund builds up with the intention of it being used in the future to cover the expenses of major works, the cost of which, payable in one go, might be beyond the tenants' pockets.

If such sums are requested in advance by a landlord, under the Act the sums requested must be reasonable. For example, the request of a large sum payable in advance to cover the cost of future expenditure and maintenance would be unreasonable on a brand new block, where one would expect maintenance costs to be low for several years.

Payment for work already carried out 23.8.2

The Act provides that the work must have been completed to a satisfactory standard, or the tenant is not obliged to pay towards it.

Payment of large sums 23.8.3

Sometimes, there is no alternative to charging the tenants large sums for expensive work, eg. when no sinking fund has been maintained. The third provision deals with this.

Where such works will incur expenditure above a prescribed limit, the landlord must obtain *two estimates* for the work. The current prescribed limit is £25 multiplied by the number of flats in the building, or £500, whichever is the greater.

One of the estimates must be from someone unconnected with the landlord and each tenant is entitled to make observations to the landlord on the estimate, to which the landlord must then pay regard.

23.8.4 Further information

The last provision allows a tenant to ask for further service charge information, which they are entitled to receive from the landlord. They are also entitled to ask that it be certified by a qualified accountant unconnected with the landlord.

Self-assessment questions

1 Draft a parcels clause for a middle flat in a block of three (ground, 1st and 2nd floor).

2 What rights, eg. access, services, will that flat need over the other two flats and how many of them will need to be reciprocated? List them.

3 Why does a flat lease need mutual enforceability of covenants?

4 What are the alternative methods of ensuring that a block of flats is looked after satisfactorily? Which would you prefer if you were:

(a) a tenant;

(b) the landlord?

Chapter 24

The assignment of a registered lease

Introduction 24.1

Where title to leasehold property has been registered, the assignment of the lease is basically a sale of registered land. The steps taken in the transaction are, therefore, almost identical to the steps taken in purchasing freehold registered land. There are, however, some *extra* matters which need to be considered because the property is leasehold.

Note

Throughout this and the next chapter, this companion will refer to 'sellers' and 'buyers'. 'Seller' means the *assignor* of the lease and 'buyer' means the *assignee* of the lease. The sale of any existing leases is an assignment of that lease from the current leaseholder (seller) to a new leaseholder (buyer).

If no mention is made of a particular stage of the conveyancing process (for example pre-exchange searches), you may assume that the procedure for leasehold land is identical to the freehold procedure. In order, the stages are:

- Taking instructions;
- Drafting the contract and deducing the title;
- Making pre-contract searches and enquiries;
- Approving the contract;
- Investigating title;
- Preparing the purchase deed;
- Preparing for completion;
- Making pre-completion searches;
- Completion;
- Post-completion.

Taking instructions 24.2

Consent to assignment 24.2.1

The seller's solicitor will need to take additional instructions from their client because of the provisions of the lease.

The lease may contain a *qualified prohibition* against assignment, eg. the lease cannot be assigned without the consent in writing of the landlord, such consent is called a 'licence to assign'. If so, the landlord's requirements regarding the information to be provided before they will give consent must be ascertained at the earliest possible stage and complied with.

Note

No money can be charged by the landlord for giving such consent although the landlord's legal fees are usually payable by the tenant.

The consent should be established before exchange of contracts. Standard Condition 8.3 stipulates that where such consent is required by the lease the seller will use all reasonable efforts to obtain it by completion and that if it is not given, or it is given subject to a condition to which the buyer reasonably objects, rescission will be available to either party. To exchange contracts in the hope that it will be forthcoming by the completion date would be foolhardy, and if all reasonable efforts have not been made the seller will be liable for breach of contract.

24.2.2 Other documents

The following items will also have to be provided to the buyer's solicitor and therefore need to be obtained from the seller:

- A receipt for the last ground rent payable;
- Details of insurance covering the property;
- Details of the last three years' service charge accounts (where payable and assuming the property is at least three years old).

If the client is unable to provide these from their own records, copies must be obtained from the landlord, or managing agent, or management company. As no prudent buyer will exchange contracts for the purchase of the property until all these items have been provided, it is important that they are collated at an early stage in the transaction. They must therefore be requested when taking instructions.

24.3 Drafting the contract and deducing title

This is done by the *seller's solicitor.*

In addition to the usual description of the property being sold, the description will also need to make reference to the number of years unexpired on the lease (the residue of the term).

As in freehold conveyancing, the covenants for title which will be given by the seller in the transfer will need to be specified in the contract (*see* Chapter 8, para. 8.6). Whether the transfer is made with full or with limited title guarantee, there are certain additional covenants which are implied in a disposition of leasehold land. Section 4(1), Law of Property (Miscellaneous Provisions) Act 1994 implies covenants that:

(a) The lease is subsisting at the time of the disposition;

(b) There is no subsisting breach of a condition or tenant's obligation, and nothing which at that time would render the lease liable to forfeiture.

However, SC 3.2.2 provides that leasehold property is sold subject to any subsisting breach of a condition or tenant's obligation relating to the physical state of the property which renders the lease liable to forfeiture. If this contractual provision is followed through in the transfer (*see* 24.7), the buyer will then have no recourse to the seller if it later appears that a past failure to repair or decorate has rendered the lease liable for forfeiture – another example of the maxim *caveat emptor* in practice.

A copy of the lease will be sent to the buyer's solicitor with the draft contract.

Deducing title 24.3.1

Where title is registered, the rules are the same as in freehold conveyancing. The open contract rule is contained in s.110, Land Registration Act 1925 but the Standard Conditions of Sale improve upon that section by requiring the provision of office copies as opposed to mere copies of the entries on the Register. The requirement in s.110 that the seller must supply 'evidence of matters as to which the Register is not conclusive' means that a copy of the lease must also be supplied.

Title may be registered with absolute leasehold, good leasehold or possessory leasehold title.

If the title is absolute, the only evidence of title a buyer can (or would want to) require are office copies of the entries on the Register of that leasehold title and a copy of the lease.

If the title is less than absolute, ie. good leasehold or possessory, neither the open contract rule nor the standard conditions of sale entitle the buyer to anything more than this. However, if a seller is in possession of any evidence of the superior title a buyer will certainly want to see it, in the hope that it may be sufficient to enable them to upgrade the title. In such cases the seller's solicitor has to think carefully about what superior title (if any) the seller can deduce and make it quite clear to the buyer by means of a special condition in the contract that this is all that will be available.

24.4 Making pre-contract enquiries

The property information form contains additional enquiries relating specifically to leasehold properties. Before contracts are exchanged the buyer's solicitor will want to see that satisfactory replies have been given to all these and that documentary evidence supporting such statements has been provided, eg. regarding service charge amounts.

The lease may contain a qualified (or absolute) *prohibition* against additions or alterations to the property. If so, information should be sought from the seller as to whether any additions or alterations have been made since the lease was granted and, if so, evidence of the landlord's consent will need to be supplied by the seller.

Other searches and enquiries will be the same as those for a freehold purchase.

24.5 Approving the contract

The buyer's solicitor will need to consider all the terms of the contract, as in freehold conveyancing.

The terms of the lease will also need careful consideration. When taking an assignment of an existing lease it is extremely *unlikely* that a buyer's solicitor will seek amendments to that lease. Amendments simply improving upon the general structure, wording, style, etc. of a lease, once it has already been granted, are not necessary or appropriate – the lease may not be perfect in your opinion, but changing leases is rare.

Sometimes a lease must be changed because it contains a wholly unacceptable clause, eg. a *forfeiture for bankruptcy clause*. In such circumstances a *deed of variation* will be needed to alter the lease. This has to be agreed between the current tenant (the seller) and the landlord before exchange of contracts and executed by them before completion. The landlord may or may not agree to do this, the option is theirs. They may well need monetary persuasion. If they do not, the buyer will probably not proceed with the purchase.

If the title is anything less than absolute, the buyer's solicitor may want to insist upon a special condition in the contract requiring the seller to deduce the *superior* title, evidence of which can then be forwarded to the Registrar with an application for the title to be upgraded.

Note

No application for upgrading good leasehold title to absolute can be made without supplying sufficient evidence to satisfy the Registrar on all superior titles.

Whether or not a seller's solicitor is able to agree to such a special condition will entirely depend upon the title evidence they have available. Even if a seller is unable to supply sufficient evidence of title to enable upgrading to take place, it is in the buyer's interest to inspect whatever evidence can be provided and a special condition will need to be inserted into the contract to enable them to do this.

If such evidence cannot be provided then the buyer and any prospective mortgagee need to be warned of the implications of less than absolute title.

Investigating title 24.6

Where the title is absolute, the procedure is identical to that undertaken in freehold conveyancing.

Where the title is less than absolute, whatever superior title the seller is able to provide must be investigated in the same way as if that title itself were being purchased. For example, if the superior title were unregistered freehold, you would adopt the same procedure as if you were buying the unregistered freehold title and you would look at all the documents supplied and raise any necessary requisitions on them.

Preparing the purchase deed 24.7

This will be a Land Registry Form 19 (or Form 19 JP if there are joint purchasers). This is prepared in exactly the same way as in freehold conveyancing but will include a specific provision to limit the implied covenants for title as provided for by SC 3.2.2 (*see* 24.3). The following words will therefore be incorporated into the transfer (normally in the space at the foot of the front page).

This transfer is made with [full/limited] title guarantee but excluding from that guarantee the covenant set out in s.4(1)(b), Law of Property (Miscellaneous Provisions) Act 1994.

Preparing for completion 24.8

In addition to the normal preparations for the sale of registered freehold land, there will be other things to consider.

24.8.1 Seller's solicitor

You will need to:

- Prepare a *completion statement* which takes account additionally of any apportionment of ground rent, service charges, etc. which are payable on the property;
- Ensure that *receipts* for all sums claimed in that statement are available to be handed over on completion;
- Ensure the landlord's duly executed *consent* is available by completion, if this is needed.

24.8.2 Buyer's solicitor

The completion statement containing the apportionments needs to be carefully checked.

24.9 Making pre-completion searches

If the title is absolute the searches will be identical to those undertaken for freehold registered land.

If the title is less than absolute and any superior title has been deduced, searches will need to be carried out in relation to that title, ie. if it is registered – Land Registry searches, if it is unregistered – land charges searches against known estate owners for the period of their ownership.

24.10 Completion

24.10.1 What the buyer must receive

On completion the buyer must receive:

- *Land certificate* (or charge certificate if the property is mortgaged);
- If the property is mortgaged, *Form 53* (or a satisfactory undertaking in respect of the same and the handing over of a duly completed Form 53 at a later date);
- *Transfer*, duly executed;
- Original *lease*;
- Duplicate *notices of assignment* relating to past transactions, if appropriate;
- The original of the *ground rent receipt*. Although it if far more preferable to receive this, if the seller has reason to retain the original, at the very least it must be available for inspection on completion so that any copy given to the buyer can be marked as having been so examined.

Note

When a landlord has issued a clear ground rent receipt, it raises a presumption that the landlord has accepted that all the covenants in the lease have been complied with: s.42(2), Law of Property Act 1925. This protects the buyer as far as possible against action by the landlord for forfeiture for non-compliance by the seller with leasehold covenants.

Other documents 24.10.2

In *some cases* the buyer must also receive:

- The *landlord's consent* – where the lease provides that this is required before it can be assigned. Evidence of consent takes the form of a duly executed *licence to assign*.
- Evidence of *service charge payments* where these are payable under the lease. Either the receipts must be handed over or the originals made available for inspection.
- Originals of whatever *superior title* has been deduced if the title is less than absolute. You must inspect and mark your abstract or epitome of that title as having been so examined.
- The *share certificate* and a *transfer* of the share if the property has the benefit of a share in a residents' company (if the company is limited by shares and not by guarantee).

Post-completion 24.11

Stamping 24.11.1

If the price being paid for the property exceeds the *ad valorem* stamp duty limit (currently £60,000) then *ad valorem* stamp duty will need to be paid on that consideration at the rate of 1%.

Note

It is the transfer document itself, not the lease, which is stamped following an assignment of an existing lease.

If the original lease term is seven years or more, a PD Form must be completed.

Registration 24.11.2

As this is registered land, the dealing has to be submitted for registration in precisely the same way and using the same forms as if this were a registered freehold title. The lease itself is only submitted to the Land Registry when the lease is registered for the first time, and it will not need to be sent when the application is only to register a transfer of an existing lease.

24.11.3 Notice to the landlord

If the lease contains a clause requiring notice to be given to the landlord of any assignment (and/or mortgage), this must be done.

Note

Where notice is required of both assignments and mortgages, this will require the service of two notices *and* the payment of two fees to the landlord.

24.11.4 Custody of documents

Once the:

- *Registration* of the transaction has been completed at the Land Registry;
- The *land or charge certificate* has been checked by the buyer's solicitor; and
- The landlord has returned duplicates of the *notices* served in accordance with the terms of the lease;

these items, together with the:

- *Original lease*; and
- All other *documents relating to the property* which will be needed on any future sale;

have to be held somewhere for *safe custody*.

If the property is not mortgaged, you need to take instructions from the client concerning the destination of the deeds. If it is mortgaged, they will be sent to the mortgagee.

Self-assessment questions

1 List the searches and enquiries you would make throughout the transaction if the title being sold were absolute.
2 What is a licence to assign and when would you need it?
3 Why is a ground rent receipt needed?
4 When is a notice of assignment given, and by whom?

Chapter 25

The assignment of an unregistered lease

Introduction 25.1

The stages involved in the assignment of an unregistered lease are the same as those involved in the assignment of a registered lease:

- Taking instructions;
- Drafting the contract and deducing the title;
- Making pre-contract searches and enquiries;
- Approving the contract;
- Investigating title;
- Preparing the purchase deed;
- Preparing for completion;
- Making pre-completion searches;
- Completion;
- Post-completion.

Taking instructions 25.2

The instructions that the seller's solicitor takes from the client when selling unregistered leasehold are no different from the points that need to be considered where the title is already registered (*see* Chapter 24, para. 24.2).

Drafting the contract and deducing title 25.3

The contract is drafted by the seller's solicitor.

Particulars of the lease 25.3.1

Particulars of the lease, and reference to the number of years outstanding on it, are the same as in registered leasehold title.

Deducing title 25.3.2

The open contact rule
Conditions relating to what title has to be shown will be different where the title is unregistered.

The open contract rule, which is unaltered by the Standard Conditions of Sale, provides that if the title to the lease is unregistered, a buyer is entitled to see the lease itself and all assignments and other dispositions, eg. assents to beneficiaries, under which it has been held during the 15 years prior to the contract date. If the lease has not been in existence for 15 years, a buyer will be entitled to see all the assignments and other dispositions of the lease that have taken place. Under the open contract rule the buyer is not entitled to see any superior title.

If, as is very likely, the term still to run on the lease exceeds 21 years, the buyer will need to apply for *first registration* of the lease following completion. The buyer will want to register the lease with absolute leasehold title as anything inferior is considerably less marketable. In order to obtain absolute leasehold title the buyer will need to satisfy the Registrar on all superior title. It is clear, therefore, that the unaltered open contract rule will be *wholly unacceptable* to a buyer in this position.

Special conditions

For this reason, every buyer will want to see a special condition providing for *deduction of title* to enable them to register with absolute leasehold title. If a seller is able to deduce title in this way, the contract should be drafted with such a condition in it.

If, however, the seller is not in a position to deduce all *superior title* in this way, then this also should be made clear by a special condition in the contract, detailing what title (if any) the seller is able to deduce and making it clear that no further requisitions or objections will be allowed from the buyer on this point.

25.4 Making pre-contract searches and enquiries

These will be the same as where the lease is registered (*see* Chapter 24, para. 24.4) with the addition of a public index map search.

25.5 Approving the draft contract

The points which need to be considered here are the same as where the lease being sold is registered, with the exception of the conditions relating to deducing title (*see* para. 25.3.2).

A buyer will need to seek the best possible evidence of superior title which, in effect, means having deduced to the buyer the superior title in exactly the same way as if that title itself were being purchased. Anything less than this is likely to mean that the application for first registration will result in title which is less than absolute being granted.

If such title cannot be deduced and the grant of an inferior class of title is predictable, the client and any prospective mortgagee must be fully informed of the consequences of this, before exchange.

Investigating title 25.6

Whatever title has been deduced to the buyer it will need to be investigated in exactly the same way as if it were that title itself being purchased. If the lease being purchased was granted out of the freehold, then the freehold title needs to be investigated using the same procedures as apply to the purchase of freehold land.

In addition, changes in ownership of the lease being purchased will need to be examined, again applying the same principles and procedures as those applying in freehold land.

If the lease being sold is not the first to have been granted out of the freehold, and has itself been granted out of a lease, then that 'superior' lease, and all changes in ownership of it for the past 15 years (if possible) will need to be investigated in the same way.

Note

The rules for investigating title and the principles you apply will be familiar, but the investigation will need to be more extensive in respect of unregistered leasehold land as there will be more 'levels' of title to be checked.

Preparing the purchase deed 25.7

This will take the form of a deed of assignment. The clauses to be contained in an assignment reflect very closely those contained in a conveyance with the following differences.

Recitals clause 25.7.1

The recitals clause will refer to the lease and the various assignments and other dispositions that have been made of it, tracing its history from the original grant of the lease to the present day. The fact that there has been an agreement between the parties for the sale of the lease will be recited and, if the lease requires a licence to assign from the landlord, this will also be stated in the recitals clause.

Habendum clause 25.7.2

The *habendum* clause will need to refer to the years still to run on the lease and state that the unexpired term will now vest in the buyer.

25.7.3 Indemnity covenants

Section 77, Law of Property Act 1925 provides that on the assignment of a lease for value the assignee impliedly covenants to pay the rent, to observe and perform the covenants in the lease and to indemnify the assignor against non-observance or non-performance of those covenants.

Because of the effect of s.77, no specific indemnity covenants need to be stated in an assignment of a lease for value, but if the assignment is dealt with in any other way, eg. a gift, and the assignor requires these covenants, they will need to be specifically stated.

Note

In the transfer of a registered lease such a covenant is not necessary because s.24(1)(b), LRA implies it whether value is given or not.

25.8 Preparing for completion

The same considerations apply here as where the title to the lease is unregistered (*see* Chapter 24, para. 24.8).

25.9 Making pre-completion searches

Central land charges searches will need to be made against the owner of the lease and, if they are different (for example, on a sale by a mortgagee), the seller and also against the landlord at the time of the sale. Land charges searches will also need to be made against previous owners of the lease whose names have been revealed during the deduction and investigation of title procedure for the period of their ownership.

Where the freehold title has been deduced, land charges searches will also need to be carried out against the names of previous estate owners of the freehold title for the period of their ownership.

Thus, the principles used to decide which names should be searched against are the same as in freehold conveyancing, but the searches are likely to be against considerably more names because the title being sold is leasehold.

25.10 Completion

25.10.1 What the buyer must receive

The buyer must receive:

- The *original lease*;

- All *assignments* and other dispositions of that lease;
- The *assignment in favour of the buyer*, duly executed;
- If the property is mortgaged, the *receipted mortgage deed* or a *satisfactory undertaking* to supply it later;
- Duplicate *notices of assignment* if the lease requires this;
- Where the superior title has been deduced, the buyer's solicitor must inspect the originals at completion and prepare a *marked abstract* of the superior title.
- The original of the *ground rent receipt* (or, at the very least, be able to inspect it).

Other documents 25.10.2

These are as detailed in Chapter 24, para. 24.10.2 – which you should revise now.

Post-completion 25.11

The assignment 25.11.l

The assignment itself will need to be stamped. The principles to be applied in stamping of an assignment are the same as applied to the stamping of a transfer (*see* Chapter 24, para. 24.11.l).

Land Registry 25.11.2

Unless there are less than 21 years left to run on the lease which has been assigned, it will need to be registered following completion. Where the superior title is unregistered, this will constitute a *first* registration and the same rules as to time limits apply as for first registration of freehold land (*see* Chapter 17, para. 17.2.3 and Chapter 22, para. 22.5.2).

The documents which need to be delivered will be not only those relating to the lease itself, but also all evidence relating to the superior title, in the form of abstracts or epitomes which have been marked as having been examined against the originals.

Notice to landlord and custody of documents 25.11.3

These matters are covered in Chapter 24, paras. 24,11.3–4 – which you should revise now.

Self-assessment questions

1 What title is a seller obliged to deduce to a buyer under the Standard Conditions of Sale?

2 Will a buyer find these conditions acceptable? If not, why not?
3 What searches will a buyer make pre-contract and pre-completion?
4 What is the time limit for registration following completion and what would be the consequences of failing to meet it?

Appendix

This Appendix contains brief details of statutes which significantly affect leasehold conveyancing. They do not form part of the Legal Practice Course, and therefore are not examinable, but we feel that they need to be included to make this companion more useful to you when you are in practice. The statutes are covered in chronological order.

Leasehold Reform Act 1967

This Act grants to tenants of long leases the right, in specified circumstances, either to acquire the freehold of their property *or* to extend their lease by 50 years.

To qualify for this right:

- The lease term must exceed 21 years and be at a low rent;
- The property must be a house – the Act does *not* apply to flats;
- The tenant must have occupied the property as their only or main residence for the last three years or three out of the last 10 years.

If the above conditions are met, there is a set procedure laid down by the Act which must be followed before tenants can avail themselves of their rights under the Act.

Landlord and Tenant Act 1987

This Act gives tenants in blocks of flats the right of first refusal should their landlord wish to dispose of its interest in the building. 'Disposal' is defined fully in the Act but includes sale – and the Act is most commonly invoked in the context of a sale.

In these circumstances the landlord has a duty to inform tenants of the proposed disposal and its terms. The tenants then have a limited time in which to decide to acquire their landlord's interest on those terms or negotiate others. A majority decision of the tenants is required.

If terms can be agreed, disposal takes place to the tenants' nominee

If no agreement is reached within the time limit, the landlord can dispose of its interests to anyone, but not at less than the original price (for the next 12 months).

There is no penalty on landlords for failing to notify tenants in the required way *but* any *new* landlord must comply and could be forced to dispose of its interest to the tenants *after* having acquired it.

Leasehold Reform, Housing and Urban Development Act 1993

Similar in its terms to the Leasehold Reform Act 1967, this Act gives rights to tenants of flats to:

- Purchase the freehold jointly (collective enfranchisement); or
- Individually extend their leases by 90 years.

The qualifying conditions and methods of assenting rights are analogous to those in the Leasehold Reform Act 1967 (save that the property does not have to be a house).

Landlord and Tenant Covenants Bill (1995/96)

At the time of publication, this Bill was not in force. It deals primarily with commercial leases. The Act limits the ongoing liability of original tenants of commercial leases so that certain steps must be taken if liability on such leases is to extend beyond the current tenants.